W9-BLR-693

GENOMICS

A Revolution in Health and Disease Discovery

Whitney Stewart and
Hans C. Andersson, MD

TWENTY-FIRST CENTURY BOOKS / MINNEAPOLIS

We dedicate this book to patients with inherited disorders whose diagnostic odyssey is years long and often ends in unsatisfactory treatments. We also hope our book will inspire young readers to train in the field of genetic science and medicine where they can dedicate their life to unraveling the mysteries of the genome.

Acknowledgments: The authors would like to thank William Gahl, clinical director of the National Human Genome Research Institute and director of the Undiagnosed Diseases Program, for his time and expertise. We also thank Anne Sophia Everett for reading an early draft and offering feedback. We are grateful to the patients and their family members who generously took time to answer our questions. We have changed their names to protect privacy.

Twenty-First Century Book
An imprint of Lerner Publishing Group, Inc.
241 First Avenue North
Minneapolis, MN 55401 USA

For reading levels and more information, look up this title at www.lernerbooks.com.

Main body text set in Metro Office.
Typeface provided by Linotype AG.

Library of Congress Cataloging-in-Publication Data

Names: Stewart, Whitney, 1959– author. | Andersson, Hans Christoph, 1956– author.
Title: Genomics : a revolution in health and disease discovery / Whitney Stewart and Hans Andersson, MD.
Description: Minneapolis : Twenty-First Century Books, [2021] | Includes bibliographical references and index. | Audience: Ages 13–18 | Audience: Grades 10–12 | Summary: "Since the completion of the Human Genome Project, genetic studies has transitioned into an era of discovery. This book explores the breakthroughs in research that inform our understanding of ancestry, inheritance, epigenetics, health, and medicine." — Provided by publisher.
Identifiers: LCCN 2019041514 (print) | LCCN 2019041515 (ebook) | ISBN 9781541500563 (library binding) | ISBN 9781728401560 (ebook)
Subjects: LCSH: Genomics.
Classification: LCC QH447 .S74 2021 (print) | LCC QH447 (ebook) | DDC 572.8/6—dc23

LC record available at https://lccn.loc.gov/2019041514
LC ebook record available at https://lccn.loc.gov/2019041515

Manufactured in the United States of America
1-43699-33491-2/4/2020

INTRODUCTION

Roy remembers being a healthy child despite suffering from a sinus infection about once a year. Back then Roy had more important things to think about than head congestion and a runny nose. He was a talented trumpet player and started playing in nightclubs at the age of fourteen. Later, though, he began to have more frequent sinus infections and often felt tired. He thought his health problems came from performing at night in a smoke-filled room and from not getting enough sleep.

Roy's fatigue grew worse, so he went to the doctor. He was diagnosed with iron-deficiency anemia, or a low red blood cell count, which can make people tired, lightheaded, and weak. Treatment for iron-deficiency anemia usually involves taking iron supplements and eating a diet rich in iron and vitamins needed to make red blood cells. Roy was under medical care, but his anemia persisted. He still felt weak and continued to have sinus infections. When he was twenty, Roy had sinus surgery, but that didn't cure his infections. After college, despite having health issues, Roy toured as a musician, taught music classes, and gave trumpet lessons on the side. His schedule was demanding, so it was hard to tell if his fatigue came from his busy lifestyle, anemia, infections, or from something else.

Roy went to graduate school to earn his doctorate degree in music. In his late twenties he started to feel more extreme fatigue. He couldn't understand it because he was getting more sleep than he had when he was a touring musician. He also had regular stomach upset and chronic diarrhea. His lymph nodes became swollen, which is a sign of inflammation in the body. Roy went to a gastroenterologist because of his intestinal trouble, and this time, he was diagnosed with celiac disease, an autoimmune disorder. In patients with autoimmune disorders, the immune system mistakenly attacks healthy cells in the body. When people with celiac disease eat gluten—a protein in wheat, rye, and barley—their body triggers an immune response that damages the small intestine. Without treatment, a person with celiac disease can develop such serious health problems as type 1 diabetes, multiple sclerosis, and intestinal cancer. People with celiac must avoid eating gluten found in such common foods as traditional spaghetti, ramen, pizza, batter-fried chicken, bread, pancakes, cereal, crackers, and even soy sauce.

What did this mean for Roy? He had to change his diet. "I hoped that going gluten-free would be easy, and I'd be fine." But his new diet didn't help. He still had chronic diarrhea and was using the restroom about a dozen times a day. And his lymph nodes continued to swell, sometimes to the size of a golf ball. Roy's doctors removed and tested his lymph nodes, but the pathology tests came back negative for obvious causes. They could not figure out what was making Roy so sick.

By the time Roy was in his early thirties, he had seen so many medical specialists he couldn't count them all— gastroenterologists, dermatologists, immunologists, and hematologists. Sometimes he could barely drag himself out of bed. "I felt useless," he said.

Something was causing all of Roy's symptoms, but none of his doctors knew how to identify it. Other members of Roy's family had autoimmune disorders: type 1 diabetes, which affects blood sugar levels, and Crohn's disease, which causes inflammation in the intestinal track. Roy's mother died when she was only forty-three after having suffered from a persistent and undiagnosed intestinal problem. Could it be that Roy and his family members suffered from an undiagnosed genetic disorder that was passed down through generations?

When Roy was born, doctors did not have nearly as many genetic tools to diagnose and treat disease. Scientists had discovered the structure of DNA but were only just beginning to identify specific genes that cause disease. In the past forty years, so much progress has been made in genetics that doctors have encountered a different problem: keeping up with the latest discoveries in the field and using new information in patient care. New diagnostic and therapeutic tools are prompting a reevaluation of all diseases. Specialists in every field are asking themselves how genetic sequencing and gene therapy can help them to understand and treat their patients.

This book follows several medical cases like Roy's that require the expertise of doctors from many specialties, who all benefit from the rapidly changing field of genetic medicine. Readers will learn about the history of genetics, how genetic mutations pass from parents to children and how these can be evaluated by such modern scientific techniques as Sanger sequencing and next-generation sequencing, and about the medical and ethical questions surrounding such services as direct-to-consumer genetic testing, gene therapy, and gene editing.

The world is still at the beginning of a paradigm shift in experts' understanding of the role of genes in medicine. This shift is advancing the field of genomics, an area within genetics

Genetic researchers use a slew of tools to assist with their experiments, including test tubes, pipettes, and microscopes. Many of the tools are the same ones used in high school chemistry classes.

concerned with the structure, function, and editing of genomes. Whereas the field of genetics is about heredity and genetic variation, genomics explores an organism's entire genome. As such, health care requires a firm knowledge of current advances in genetics, including genomics. This book will bring the reader up to date in the most rapidly changing field of medicine and equip readers with the knowledge to make sense of daily news stories about gene therapy and personalized medicine. Twenty-first-century genetics is changing how people define themselves and understand their health, and it informs the way doctors target disease treatment for patients with complex illnesses like Roy's.

CHAPTER 1
UNDIAGNOSED DISEASES

For most of his life, Roy has lived and worked through repeated illnesses and recovery. A group of medical specialists took on his case, but they had trouble finding one diagnosis to explain all of his symptoms. An immunologist eventually diagnosed Roy with common variable immune deficiency (CVID), a disorder that impairs the immune system. Patients with CVID have a low level of antibodies, proteins in the blood that fight off infection. Although the word *common* is in the name of the disease, only about one in twenty-five thousand people have this medical condition. Patients don't all have the same symptoms, but they often suffer from chronic bacterial infections in the sinuses, ears, lungs, and gastrointestinal track. They may also have swollen lymph nodes and spleen. About 25 percent of patients with CVID also have an autoimmune disorder, as Roy does.

Doctors believe that the cause of CVID is a combination of genetics (an inherited condition) and environment. The environmental causes are unclear but can include a patient's life experiences, diet, exercise, and exposure to disease. The genetic influences are caused by mutations, pathogenic (disease-causing) variants, in genes that are involved with the formation and function of B cells. When these special white blood cells mature in healthy people, they produce proteins called antibodies, or immunoglobulins, to help fight infection. In some CVID patients, however, genetic mutations can disrupt B cell function and antibody production, leading to immune dysfunction. However, only about 10 percent of CVID patients have a known genetic mutation associated with the disorder. Roy is not one of them.

Patients with CVID often have to take antibiotics and commonly receive ongoing immunoglobulin replacement therapy. Roy added this therapy to his busy schedule as a university music professor and family man (he had married and fathered two children), but he continues to get sick. He knew he had to advocate for himself and take more steps to find out what was causing his medical condition, so he applied to the Undiagnosed Diseases Program (UDP) at the National Institutes of Health (NIH).

UNDIAGNOSED DISEASES PROGRAM AND NETWORK

William Gahl, clinical director of the National Human Genome Research Institute, understands the importance of correct medical diagnoses. "Patients who have rare diseases are often abandoned by the medical community. We don't know how to treat [them] if we don't have a diagnosis," he says.

Inspired to help people who cannot find medical treatment, Gahl, who trained in pediatrics and biochemical genetics, led the creation of the Undiagnosed Diseases Program at the NIH in Bethesda, Maryland, in 2008. The UDP focuses on two goals: "To provide answers to patients with mysterious conditions that have long eluded diagnosis, and to advance medical knowledge about rare and common diseases." In its first ten years, the program received over four thousand applications, accepted

WHAT IS A GENE?

Danish botanist Wilhelm Johannsen coined the term *gene* to mean "a heritable unit," and he published this concept in his 1909 textbook. A gene is a sequence of DNA that contains the information to create a specific protein needed for the body's structure and function and for the regulation of cells, tissues, and organs. Genes also carry specific instructions for individual traits, such as hair and eye color. Genes are split into coding sequences, or exons, which produce proteins; and noncoding sequences, or introns, which do not produce proteins. The human genome contains between twenty thousand and twenty-five thousand genes.

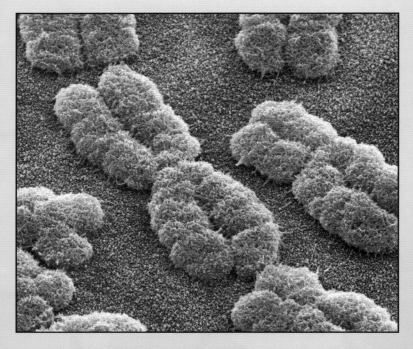

An electron micrograph of human chromosomes. Genes exist on chromosomes.

just over eleven hundred patients, and diagnosed about three hundred patients. From that work, NIH doctors discovered fifteen previously unknown diseases.

The UDP brings together a large team of ultraspecialists—leaders in their fields of medicine and human medical research—who work on the NIH campus. The NIH is akin to a university devoted to all forms of medical research with twenty-seven individual institutes, each devoted to certain groups of diseases. For instance, the National Institute of Child Health and Human Development researches diseases in children. The UDP benefits from collaborations of clinician-scientists from all the NIH institutes.

Patients with complicated health issues can apply to the UDP for a free medical consultation. Their referring doctors must send all the patient's medical records to the UDP. The program accepts only about 28 percent of applicants because of the enormous amount of resources required to investigate each patient's case. Gahl reviews the applications and examines the objective findings in the medical records. He then decides whether to show the patient's records to other NIH physicians. He may refer a complicated case to the internist or neurologist on staff, or to experts in fields such as immunology, rheumatology, or hematology who work at NIH. The doctors at NIH use advanced medical tools, including blood tests, scans, and genetic testing to help figure out the causes of their patients' disorders. And they suggest clinical treatment whenever possible. Gahl believes that by understanding the rare diseases of participants in the program, doctors might also learn something new about diseases that are more common.

The UDP has been so important to research and to clinical care that in 2013, it expanded into a network of programs, the Undiagnosed Diseases Network (UDN), at seven university

William Gahl helped create the Undiagnosed Diseases Program, which examines patients with unique and particularly confounding symptoms. The UDP utilizes genetic research to help identify previously unknown genetic mutations that may give rise to patients' conditions.

medical centers. And in 2018, it added five more sites. The coordinating center for this network is at the Department of Biomedical Informatics at Harvard Medical School in Massachusetts. At each clinical site, doctors from many specialties come together to try to solve the medical mystery of each patient.

Patients who apply to the UDN often see this as their last hope. Many of them have disorders that doctors have never seen before. UDN clinicians cannot guarantee they will be able to cure their patient's suffering, but they do their best to address the symptoms. As Gahl has said, "We make it pretty clear to the patients that we're not making any commitments to find a treatment for them. But, in fact, we're still doctors, and we still try."

Often one of the most important things to a patient with a confusing illness—and to the patient's family—is just to get

WHAT IS GENETIC TESTING?

Doctors order genetic testing to help patients understand their chances of having or developing a genetic disorder or passing it on to their children. The results can confirm or rule out a suspected gene variant that contributes to disease.

According to the National Institutes of Health's Genetic Home Reference page, there are three different types of genetic testing:

- Molecular genetic tests (or gene tests) study single genes or short lengths of DNA to identify variations or mutations that lead to a genetic disorder.
- Chromosomal genetic tests analyze whole chromosomes or long lengths of DNA to see if there are large genetic changes, such as an extra copy of a chromosome, that cause a genetic condition.
- Biochemical genetic tests study the amount or activity level of proteins; abnormalities in either can indicate changes to the DNA that result in a genetic disorder.

a diagnosis. A confirmed diagnosis gives the patient some certainty of understanding the problem even when a treatment is unknown. Also, if doctors can identify other patients who have the same gene mutations and medical conditions, the patients and their families can form an alliance to help educate one another and their communities. Such alliances, often formed via Facebook groups or other social media, can be a source of support for affected patients and their family members.

STILL UNDIAGNOSED

When Roy was thirty-two, the Undiagnosed Diseases Program at the NIH accepted him as a patient. "Getting accepted into the UDP was a huge deal," he said. "I felt so fortunate. And they

66 Not knowing what's wrong with you is so frustrating. Sometimes doctors can't find answers on their tests, and they dismiss your medical case. When that happens, you wonder if you are a hypochondriac. But you still feel lousy and don't know where to turn. Patients have to do their own research, ask questions, and seek another doctor. My diagnosis took years. I saw gastroenterologists, rheumatologists, sinus specialists, even acupuncturists. Finally, one immunologist was willing to look beyond the obvious and test me for immune deficiency. That was it!"

—Sydney, immune deficiency patient

flew me to the NIH and did so many tests and scans." Roy has returned to the NIH many times because his medical condition is complicated and interests the doctors there. Through magnetic resonance imaging (MRI), doctors discovered brain and spine lesions, or abnormal tissue, that they want to follow more closely. Roy hadn't noticed any problems in his spine, but he had experienced headaches. Doctors told him they knew what to look for because such inflammation was common in their patients with immune and autoimmune disorders. CVID patients commonly have granulomas (masses of immune cells) that form at sites of inflammation or infection. Roy found out his immune cells are attacking his brain and spine, and also his lungs, kidneys, and eyes.

Even after years of visiting the NIH, Roy still hasn't received a firm diagnosis. His NIH immunologist says Roy has immunodeficiency, but she can't yet be more specific about

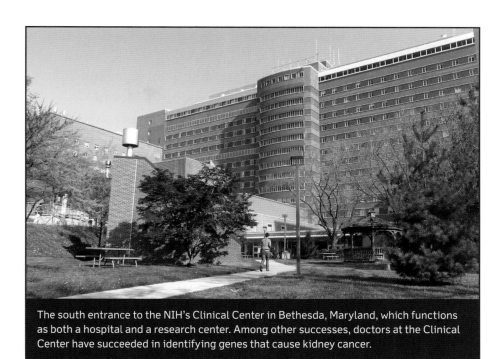

The south entrance to the NIH's Clinical Center in Bethesda, Maryland, which functions as both a hospital and a research center. Among other successes, doctors at the Clinical Center have succeeded in identifying genes that cause kidney cancer.

his illness. She prescribed a corticosteroid to reduce Roy's inflammation and keep his immune system from attacking itself. And Roy has to have infusions of another immunosuppressant drug, a targeted therapy for tumors. On his new treatment, Roy feels better but experiences side effects of arthritis-like symptoms. His lymph nodes have shrunk, and his energy level improved. But taking drugs that suppress the immune system is complicated for a patient who already has a weakened immune system. The patient could easily get an infection that's hard to treat. Roy and his doctors work hard to help keep his immune system and overall health in balance—not easy with such a complicated disorder. And what about a diagnosis?

Roy's immunologist at NIH has suspected that he might have a rare genetic mutation of the cytotoxic T-lymphocyte–associated antigen-4 (*CTLA4*) gene. The *CTLA4* gene tells cells how to make

" As a patient, you're looking for a doctor who has expert knowledge of your condition. And you also want someone who has a good bedside manner. When you have both of those, it's usually rare. I have been fortunate to find folks at the NIH who have both. They take their time and say we're going to get to the bottom of this. For a young person going into health care, the NIH would be an amazing destination. It's inspiring. . . . They have all those brilliant minds in one place. It's impressive."

—Roy, professor of music, immune deficiency patient

the *CTLA4* protein, which slows down and helps control the immune system. Each person inherits two copies of the *CTLA4* gene, one from each parent. According to the National Institute of Allergy and Infectious Diseases, "People with only one properly functioning copy of *CTLA4* experience abnormal T cell activity, lower levels of healthy, antibody-producing B cells, higher levels of autoimmune B cells, and the disruption of organs by infiltrating immune cells." In other words, if Roy has a mutation in one *CTLA4* gene, his immune system would not work normally. Common symptoms of *CTLA4* deficiency are diarrhea, sinus and lung infections, swollen lymph nodes, and granulomas—all of which Roy has experienced.

At the NIH, Roy had genetic testing. His results did not show a *CTLA4* mutation, but his immunologist wonders if perhaps another gene mutation could be affecting Roy's *CTLA4* protein function. In the summer of 2019, Roy was sent to see a UDP rheumatologist who treats patients with autoimmune diseases, and he had more genetic testing. These new tests showed that

Roy has a mutation in the *HLA-B51* gene, often associated with autoimmune disorders, and particularly with Behçet's disease, which Roy does not have. That mutation, however, does not explain Roy's immunodeficiency. "I suppose that could be a good lesson in how genetics can send you down a rabbit hole trying to fit certain symptoms into a disease while searching for a definitive diagnosis," Roy said after learning the results of his latest genetic tests. He doesn't know how long NIH doctors will continue to follow his condition—perhaps until they can unravel his perplexing medical mystery.

CHAPTER 2
GENETIC CONCEPTS
THEN AND NOW

Before scientists and doctors could make a connection
between genes and illness, they first had to understand how
one generation passes down physical characteristics to the next.
Around 530 BCE, the Greek mathematician Pythagoras suggested
that inheritable traits came from the father, who transmitted
them to the human embryo in the womb. In his theory, the
mother's body transferred nutrition to the fetus but no physical
features. Later, the ancient Greek philosopher Hippocrates (ca.
460–370 BCE) made remarkable observations about inheritance
without any direct evidence or knowledge of genes. Hippocrates
believed that semen passed on the instructions for building
a human and that the womb provided the raw materials for
creating the child. Hippocrates also suggested that acquired
characteristics could be passed down. For example, an Olympic
weight lifter who developed large muscles during his lifetime
would pass down his large muscle traits to his children. The
children, in turn, would have large muscles.

Aristotle (384–322 BCE), another Greek philosopher, challenged Hippocrates's theories of inheritance. He noted that a man who is missing a left arm could still father children with two arms. How could that happen if the father had no left arm traits to pass down? Aristotle also realized that people can pass down such characteristics as graying hair or male pattern baldness that don't show up until their children become adults. Aristotle concluded that children must inherit some kind of biological information from both of their parents.

NATURAL SELECTION

Over the next two thousand years, scientists and philosophers had many ideas about heredity. Some believed that a human organism started as a preformed individual, in either the sperm or the egg, and it developed and enlarged in the womb. Others accepted the theory of epigenesis, the idea that an embryo is not preformed but develops in stages. It wasn't until the nineteenth century that two scientists, Charles Darwin and Gregor Mendel, gave the world more scientifically based theories of heredity.

English geologist and biologist Charles Darwin (1809–1882) worked on a ship, the HMS *Beagle*, which sailed to chart the waters of the South American coast in 1831. During his almost five-year voyage, Darwin collected specimens and wrote down his observations of their natural processes, which he sent back to the scientific community at Cambridge University in England, where he had studied. From his observations, Darwin recognized an important mechanism of inheritance that he called natural selection. He observed that those organisms whose physical characteristics make them best suited to survive in their natural environment reproduced more often than organisms that were less well adapted. They then passed on those physical

CELL DIVISION AND REPRODUCTION

In humans, trillions of cells divide every day. When people grow, cells divide. When you get a cut, cells divide to repair damaged tissue. When your hair falls out, new hair follicles produce replacement hair by *mitosis*. One cell becomes two. Two cells become four, and so on.

Cells divide in two ways, depending upon the type of cell. All cells except sperm and egg cells (gametes) divide by mitosis, when a single cell becomes two cells that are complete replicas of the parent cell. The daughter cells have the same number of chromosomes as the parent cell— forty-six in all. The parent and daughter cells are called *diploid* cells (they have two copies of each chromosome).

Meiosis is another way cells divide. In two steps the cells divide to create gametes. Meiosis first splits in half the number of chromosomes so that each daughter cell ends up with only one copy of each chromosome for a total of twenty-three rather than forty-six. Then *crossing over* sometimes takes place. During crossing over—also called *genetic recombination*—a portion of a chromosome sometimes breaks away and

characteristics to their offspring. Because of this, the next generation was better endowed to survive and reproduce and so on. This process, over many generations, would eventually give rise to a new species. This observation led to his theory of evolution.

In 1859 Darwin published his theory in his book *On the Origin of Species by Means of Natural Selection.* He received both praise and criticism for his revolutionary ideas, and his work ignited scientific, philosophical, and religious discussion. Later, in his 1868 book, *The Variation of Animals and Plants under Domestication*, Darwin proposed a theory of inheritance, which trades places with its other chromosome copy. Crossing over allows for genetic variation in the organism because it results in new and unique chromosome sequences.

In the next phase of meiosis, genetic information in each chromosome of each cell splits in half. The result is four daughter cells that have only one set of chromosomes. These are haploid cells. During fertilization, the haploid sperm and egg cells join, and the chromosomes of each come together in the daughter cell nucleus to create a diploid cell. These new diploid cells will then undergo mitosis to begin growing into a human embryo.

Errors that occur during mitosis or meiosis may lead to chromosome abnormalities such as trisomy 21 (also known as Down syndrome). Researchers can detect these with a karyotype test. They stain white blood cells to see the shape of a patient's chromosomes under a microscope. They can then identify any abnormalities, such as extra or missing pieces of chromosomes.

he called pangenesis. He believed that gemmules—his term for minute particles of inheritance thrown off by all cells of the body—collected in the parents' reproductive organs and combined to form an embryo. Darwin said gemmules were responsible for the transmission of human characteristics to children. He also suggested that an organism's external environment could alter gemmules in the body and that parents could pass down modified gemmules to their offspring (although he later rescinded this idea). Although Darwin's insights advanced the field of biology, they did not fully explain the mechanism of inheritance. Scientists continued to search for the substance that actually passes down from parents to children and for an explanation as to how exactly heredity happens.

HOW ARE TRAITS PASSED DOWN?

Another scientist researching at the same time as Darwin was Gregor Mendel (1822–1884). Mendel was born into a German-speaking family in what is now the Czech Republic, and as an adult, he became a Catholic monk. As a monastic teacher, Mendel spent almost a decade planting thousands of pea plants in his monastery garden and studying their heredity and evolution. He focused on seven plant traits: seed shape, seed color, pod shape, pod color, stem length, the position of the flower on the stem, and flower color. He cross-fertilized pea plants with different traits to see which would appear in the next generation. And he kept meticulous notes on his cross-pollination of seedlings. His research showed a pattern and helped him identify three laws of inheritance:

LAW OF SEGREGATION

Mendel's law of segregation dictated that each parent plant passes down to offspring a certain heritable element. In Mendel's experiment, these elements each came in two variants: white or purple flower color, tall or short stem height, round or wrinkled pea shape, yellow or green pea color, terminal or axial flower position on the stem, inflated or constricted pod shape, and yellow or green pod color. Scientists have come to understand that Mendel's heritable elements are genes, a unit of heritable information, and the variants are alleles, alternate forms of a gene.

LAW OF INDEPENDENT ASSORTMENT

Mendel also discovered a law of independent assortment. This law refers to how each trait is independent from the others.

For example, plants with purple flowers do not necessarily have wrinkled pea shapes and vice versa, because the purple flower trait and the wrinkled pea shape trait are independent from each other. (This was true in Mendel's experiments, but cell biologists later discovered that genes can occasionally be linked and inherited together.)

LAW OF DOMINANCE

Mendel's law of dominance defines dominant variants as those that appear as a trait—as a purple flower or tall stem, for example—whenever the offspring inherits one copy of the allele. Recessive variants appear as a trait only when two copies—one from each parent—are present in the offspring. So a plant that

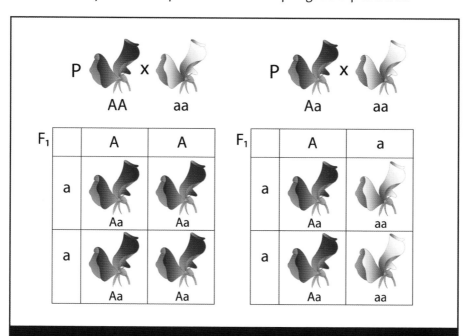

Punnett squares show how dominant and recessive phenotypes will appear in the offspring of two hypothetical parent organisms. Here, the dominant phenotypes are represented by a capital *A*, and the recessive ones by a lowercase *a*.

possesses either two dominant variants or a dominant and recessive variant will express the dominant trait. The recessive trait will only appear if the plant possesses two recessive variants.

Mendel's research focused on pea plants, but he believed his laws of inheritance to be true for all living things. In 1865 he presented his work to a small audience gathered at the Natural History Society meeting in Brno, Czech Republic (Brünn, in German), but the audience found his ideas difficult to understand. After Mendel finished his first presentation, another speaker lectured on Darwin's theory of evolution. Nobody in the audience, perhaps not even Mendel himself, seemed to make the connection between Mendel's and Darwin's research. A missed opportunity for the science world! Mendel published his research in the *Proceedings of the Natural History Society of Brünn*, but his work went mostly overlooked for decades.

Mendel went on to become the abbot of the monastery, and to his regret, he had little time for more plant experiments. "I feel truly unhappy that I have to neglect my plants and bees so completely," he wrote to a plant physiologist who he had wanted to interest in his work. Mendel died of kidney failure in 1884 without having been honored for his groundbreaking laws on inheritance that are the foundation of modern genetic theory. During Mendel's time, neither he nor other scientists ever identified the heritable element that contained and transmitted genetic material. All of their findings were based on deductive reasoning.

BIRTH OF MODERN GENETICS

The field of heredity flourished in the early twentieth century as botanists and plant breeders worked to answer questions about heredity. Dutch biologist Hugo de Vries (1848–1935), German plant geneticist Carl Correns (1864–1933), and Austrian plant breeder Erich von Tschermak-Seysenegg (1871–1962) each independently carried out experiments and reached conclusions on inheritance similar to Mendel's, effectively rediscovering Mendel's laws. They referenced Mendel's paper "Experiments on Plant Hybridization" in their own work, and this helped bring Mendel's overlooked research into prominence.

De Vries went even further, researching how genetic variants come about. He coined the term *pangene* to name heritable elements. De Vries believed species evolved from other species because of sudden changes of character traits between generations—which he called mutants, from the Latin word for "change." While working with plants called evening primroses, he observed that his plants would sometimes have offspring with significant and unique differences in leaf shape or plant size not seen in the parent plants. These offspring would then sometimes pass down these traits to the next generation. From this, he developed his theory of mutation. Unlike Darwin, who described the slow and gradual change of natural selection, de Vries believed that evolution could make dramatic jumps because of mutations, which resulted in a new species. Modern scientists know that de Vries's plants did not actually become a different species. The mutations de Vries observed were caused by spontaneous changes in genes.

As scientists throughout Europe and the United States were trying to unravel questions of heredity, one English biologist, William Bateson (1861–1926), was taking a broader look at the future of the field, which he named genetics from the Greek term *genno*, which means "to give birth." He too recognized the importance of Mendel's work and thought it so important that he translated Mendel's papers from German into English so that more scientists could read them. Bateson's recognition of Mendel's ideas helped promote Mendel as the father of genetics.

EUGENICS AND HISTORIC TRAUMA

As William Bateson reflected upon Mendel's laws of inheritance and carried out his own research on pea plants, he began to understand how people might one day misuse genetic information. Even without knowledge of DNA, Bateson was far ahead of his time when in 1928, he wrote, "What, as we asked at the outset, will happen when . . . the facts of heredity are as commonly known as those for bacteriology, for example? One thing is certain. Mankind will begin to interfere."

Bateson's writing seems to show that he foresaw the concerns people in the twenty-first century have about interfering with heredity. If Bateson had known that one day physicians could alter genes, he might have asked himself some of the questions that appear in contemporary media. Should parents, for instance, be allowed to select specific genetic traits to pass on to their children, creating a so-called "designer baby"? Should a government or national health-care system be allowed to intervene in a person's medical care if that person has a specific inherited condition? Bateson went on to write in the same passage, "When power is discovered, man always turns to it. The science of heredity will soon provide power on a stupendous scale; and in some

William Bateson was a fellow of the Royal Society, a prestigious scientific institution located in the UK. The Royal Society was first founded in 1660 and included such members as Sir Isaac Newton, Charles Darwin, Albert Einstein, and Stephen Hawking.

country, and some time, not, perhaps, far distant, that power will be applied to control the composition of a nation."

Bateson spoke out against an academic movement led by Charles Darwin's cousin, Francis Galton (1822–1911), who had studied science, medicine, and math, and had an interest in human heredity. Galton focused on eugenics (meaning "well-born"), an idea that society can be improved through controlled breeding. People with desirable traits would be encouraged to reproduce and pass on characteristics such as intelligence. People like Galton who endorsed eugenics had the mistaken idea that mental illness or intelligence traits, for example, are predictably defined by genes—as in Mendel's pea experiments. What they did not understand was that most human traits are a result of an unpredictable combination of genetics, lifestyle, and environment, and they cannot be bred out of the population.

Despite Galton's ideas being ill informed and discredited by much of the contemporary scientific community, they have had an enormous impact on millions of people. Throughout the twentieth century, eugenicists used his ideas to justify discrimination against people with disabilities, racial minorities, and anyone else who didn't fit into their "ideal" society. Their work in the United States was supported by prominent and powerful figures, such as the Rockefeller family and leaders at the Carnegie Institution. One of the founders of the Eugenics Record Office, educator Harry H. Laughlin, testified before Congress advocating forced sterilization and anti-immigration laws to control the racial profile of America. Following eugenicist principles, Congress passed the Immigration Act of 1924, which limited the number of eastern Europeans, Jews, and Arabs, and barred Asians from entering the country. Thirty-three US states, including California, Virginia, North Carolina, and Mississippi, have used forced sterilization to control minority populations. Native Americans, Asian Americans, African Americans, and Mexican Americans were among the targeted groups. And more than sixty-five thousand Americans with mental illness or developmental disabilities were sterilized between the 1920s and 1970s.

In Nazi Germany, where leader Adolf Hitler established racist and discriminating laws, the law required doctors to register any person born with a hereditary illness to the Hereditary Health Courts. Under the German Sterilization Law, starting in 1934, as many as four hundred thousand people were sterilized for such conditions as epilepsy, schizophrenia, or "feeblemindedness." Others were sterilized outside the provisions of the law for homosexuality or for belonging to a racial minority group. Germany also passed strict marriage laws that made interracial marriages and marriages between abled and disabled people illegal, as well as prevented sterilized people from marrying "healthy" people and Jewish people from marrying non-Jewish Germans. The Nazi government promoted these laws through films and advertisement, which helped create a stigma against targeted groups. The German government also allowed doctors such as Josef Mengele, who had a doctoral degree in genetic medicine, to carry out horrific and painful medical experiments on Jewish and other concentration camp prisoners, claiming their work to be in the name of genetic science.

People who endorsed eugenics subjected millions to historic trauma. Many of those whose ancestors, identities, or conditions were targeted by eugenicists are afraid that laws similar to those of the United States or Germany could pass again in the name of genetic research.

William Bateson was correct when he predicted such abuses of power to control populations. However, he continued to spread Mendel's ideas of heredity in his effort to further reputable science for the sakes of discovery and helping people, not eugenicist pseudoscience used to oppress and discriminate.

THE IMPORTANCE OF CELL BIOLOGY

In 1907 Bateson was traveling in the United States to give talks on Mendel's work when he met the cell biologist Thomas Hunt Morgan (1866–1945) in New York. Morgan became interested in determining the nature of Mendel's element of heredity, the gene, and uncovering its location within cells. He looked at past discoveries to inform how he designed his own research.

Five years earlier, in 1902, two cell biologists, Walter Sutton (1877–1916) and Theodor Boveri (1862–1915), had independently arrived at the theory that chromosomes were the carriers of genetic material. Then, in 1905, biologists Nettie Maria Stevens (1861–1912) and Edmund Beecher Wilson (1856–1939) each independently discovered sex chromosomes, and Stevens proposed that all genes might be carried on chromosomes. Morgan began his search for the gene on chromosomes.

Around 1908 Morgan planned his research using the fruit fly—the *Drosophila melanogaster*—which commonly has red eyes. In his laboratory, appropriately named the Fly Room, at Columbia University in New York, and in Woods Hole, Massachusetts, in the summer, Morgan and his students bred thousands of maggots on rotting fruit. In the stink of his fly-filled laboratory, Morgan examined the flies under his microscope. It took him until 1910 to discover a mutant fly: a male with white eyes. Morgan bred white-eyed and red-eyed flies, and he kept track of the inheritance patterns of traits through generations of flies.

Morgan made a discovery about inheritance that differed from Mendel's theory of independent assortment. Morgan discovered that in the first generation of offspring, the white-eyed flies were all males. In later generations, white-eyed females appeared. That meant that the gene for the white-eyed trait was linked to the X chromosome—the trait appeared in male flies first because they only needed to possess the gene on their single X chromosome, while female flies would need the white-eyed gene to appear on both their X chromosomes. This was important because it told Morgan that genes could occasionally be linked together when inherited, something that Mendel did not report. And if genes were linked, Morgan theorized, they must appear in similar locations on a chromosome. This idea is called genetic linkage.

Morgan made other discoveries too. He noticed that very rarely, linked genes could become unlinked and that parts of different chromosomes could trade places with one another. He called this *crossing over*. He eventually discovered that genetic information sometimes mixed or recombined over subsequent generations. From his observations of linkage, Morgan determined that genes that had no linkage must be on different chromosomes. By documenting how often offspring inherited certain traits together, he could determine how close together the corresponding genes were on a chromosome. Morgan's research was so essential to the field of genetics that he won the Nobel Prize in 1933.

Other scientists of the time were wondering whether they could actually cause gene mutations in flies. In 1926 Hermann Joseph Muller (1890–1967), an American geneticist, exposed flies to heavy doses of X-rays and looked for any effects. He then mated the exposed flies with nonexposed ones, and their offspring showed a huge variety of mutations. Under a microscope, Muller could see different chromosomal abnormalities caused by the X-rays. He proved that factors from an organism's environment could cause gene mutation. The study of how environmental factors change gene expression or activity is *epigenetics*.

DNA'S DOUBLE HELIX STRUCTURE

By the 1940s geneticists and biologists had a better idea of where to find genes within cells, how to identify inheritance patterns, and how environmental exposures could cause genetic mutations. They could also see chromosome abnormalities under a microscope but still could not describe the actual molecule that carried genetic information.

In 1944 physician and bacteriologist Oswald Avery (1877–1955), along with his colleagues Colin MacLeod (1909–1972) and Maclyn McCarty (1911–2005), advanced the field of genetics when they experimented with bacteria and discovered that a molecule in cells, deoxyribonucleic acid, or DNA, was a carrier of complex information—a so-called transforming substance. What they had uncovered and what future research confirmed was that DNA was the carrier of genetic information. The next step was to uncover the structure of DNA, which could help scientists understand its overall nature. Four scientists distinguished themselves by working to solve this mystery: biophysicist Maurice Wilkins (1916–2004), chemist and X-ray crystallographer Rosalind Franklin (1920–1958), and molecular biologists James Watson (1928–) and Francis Crick (1916–2004).

In 1946 Wilkins, the assistant director of a new Biophysics Unit at King's College in London, began using X-ray crystallography to take shadow images of DNA. Wilkins's first X-ray images, however, were blurry because of the wet nature of

66 This technique can reveal the hidden atomic structure of matter in its crystalline form. Atoms are too small to see under light microscopes, so crystallographers shoot invisible X-rays at them, which then bounce off, or diffract, onto a detector, such as film. By applying math to the diffraction pattern, it's possible to calculate the three-dimensional form of even the most complex molecules."

—Sigourney Weaver, narrator, "DNA: Secret of Photo 51," *NOVA*, PBS

DNA. He couldn't clearly see its structure. In May 1951 Wilkins gave a scientific talk at the Zoological Station in Naples, Italy. In the audience was the ambitious twenty-three-year-old Watson. Wilkins's X-ray diffraction picture of DNA inspired Watson to focus his own scientific research on DNA structure. He joined the Cavendish Laboratory at the University of Cambridge, England, and began working with British biologist Crick, who was an old friend of Wilkins.

One of the other scientists interested in deciphering the structure of DNA was Rosalind Franklin. In 1951 Franklin joined the same unit at King's College where Wilkins had begun to analyze the structure of DNA using X-ray crystallography. She and Wilkins worked separately on different DNA samples, and she took her own crystallography images, with the assistance of her PhD student Raymond Gosling (1926–2015), and kept careful notes on DNA characteristics. She experimented with changing the humidity of the DNA samples and described two forms of DNA, wet and dry.

In November 1951 Franklin gave a lecture at King's College about her crystallography work, which Watson attended. She discussed her hypothesis that DNA had a double helix shape. Franklin had good images of DNA, but she wanted to conduct further analysis on its structure before releasing the pictures. She was also not ready to announce that she had solved the mystery of DNA's form.

The morning after attending Franklin's talk, Watson met with Crick who quizzed him on the details of Franklin's research. Watson had not taken notes but relied only on his memory, which annoyed Crick. Despite Watson's failure to take precise notes, he relayed enough information on Franklin's X-ray data that Crick felt more confident in his own belief that DNA had a double helix form. Together, Watson and Crick attempted to build a model of DNA using sticks and balls. They showed one of their early

James Watson (*left*) and Francis Crick stand with their model of the DNA molecule in 1953. Watson and Crick published the first description of the DNA structure, and their work was based partially on the research of other colleagues including Maurice Wilkins and Rosalind Franklin.

models to Franklin who pointed out where the two scientists had gone wrong. Embarrassed, Watson and Crick temporarily stopped working on DNA structure, but they never forgot that other scientists were also trying to crack the DNA code. They wanted to achieve it first.

Franklin continued her work, and in May 1952, she took one particular image, Photo 51, that would become essential to the understanding of DNA structure. This photo, looking down the long DNA molecule, showed an *X*. Franklin understood this

66 The results suggest a helical structure (which must be very closely packed) containing probably [two, three, or four] coaxial nucleic acid chains per helical unit and having the phosphate groups near the outside."

—Rosalind Franklin, official report submitted in February 1952

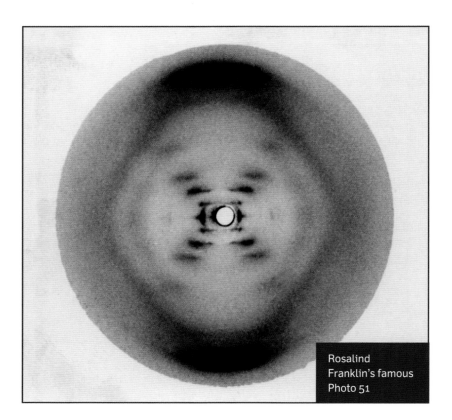

to mean that the DNA structure was indeed a double helix, a twisted ladder. She noted this in her scientific journals and filed her Photo 51 in a drawer in her laboratory.

On January 30, 1953, Watson visited the laboratory where Franklin was working. He was worried that another biochemist, Linus Pauling (1901–1994), was going to solve the problem of DNA structure before he and Crick could, so he wanted to collaborate with Wilkins and Franklin. According to Watson's memoir, he talked to Franklin, but she was not particularly interested in the physical model that he and Crick were trying to create. She was relying on her own photographs and dimensional calculations to further describe DNA. Watson left Franklin and went to find Wilkins. Later that day, Franklin was working alone behind closed doors. Wilkins took the opportunity to show Franklin's

Photo 51 to Watson without asking Franklin's permission to do so. (This story is the subject of much controversy in the history of genetics.)

"The instant I saw the picture my mouth fell open and my pulse started to race," Watson wrote in his memoir. "The pattern was unbelievably simpler than those obtained previously. . . . The black cross of reflections which dominated the pictures could arise only from a helical structure." Wilkins also said that Franklin believed DNA had a double-stranded backbone on the outside and chemical bases *on the inside*. This was crucial information because Watson and Crick had been working on a model with the bases on the outside.

This time, Watson took notes on what he had learned from Franklin's work. "I sketched on the blank edge of my newspaper what I remembered of the . . . pattern." By the time Watson was back at Cambridge, he had decided to rebuild their model of DNA.

Rosalind Franklin examines a sample under a microscope in 1955. She would pass away from cancer four years before her research helped her colleagues earn a Nobel Prize.

Franklin's Photo 51, and her research notes, which Watson also obtained without her knowing, provided the essential evidence that Watson and Crick needed to crack the code of DNA's double helix structure. They also used their own calculations based on what they understood about DNA biology to create their model. Their structure showed complementary outside strands that could open (unzip) to allow duplication of each strand in preparation for cell division. Connecting those strands were chemical compounds that paired with each other—adenine in one strand binding to thymine in the other, and guanine binding to cytosine. After working out the last of their structural problems on February 28, 1953, they went to a nearby pub, the Eagle, for lunch. There, Crick announced to anyone who cared to listen that they had discovered "the secret of life." They finished constructing their model a week later and presented it to the world in April 1953.

With the discovery of the shape of DNA, the field of genetics

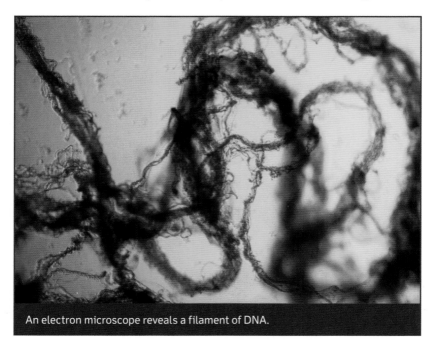

An electron microscope reveals a filament of DNA.

> **"** It [creating the DNA model] was fairly fast, but you know, we were lucky. One must remember, it was based on the X-ray work done here in London started off by Maurice Wilkins and carried on by Rosalind Franklin, and we wouldn't have got to the stage of at least having a molecular model, if it hadn't been for their work."
>
> —Francis Crick, radio interview

changed forever. These scientists published their DNA research findings—the first article by Watson and Crick, the second by Wilkins and colleagues, and a third by Franklin and Gosling—in the April 25, 1953, issue of *Nature*. Nine years later, in 1962, Watson, Crick, and Wilkins won the Nobel prize in Physiology or Medicine "for their discoveries concerning the molecular structure of nucleic acids and its significance for information transfer in living material."

Rosalind Franklin, despite her invaluable contribution, was not named in the prize. She had died four years earlier, at thirty-seven years old, of ovarian cancer.

She may never have known exactly how important her work was to the achievements of Watson, Crick, and Wilkins. It's tempting to think, however, that she would have been pleased to know her research contributed to twenty-first-century genomic medicine. Doctors know that mutations in two genes, *BRCA1* and *BRCA2*, give rise to some 15 percent of ovarian cancer diagnoses. Was Franklin's ovarian cancer caused by a mutation in her genes, or could her illness have been triggered by her exposure to X-rays? Although this question may remain unanswered, scientists and doctors would have never understood the genetic causes of cancer and other diseases without the work of Watson, Crick, Wilkins, and Franklin. Breaking the code of DNA was the catalyst for a new era of molecular biology that has begun to inform the field of medicine.

CHAPTER 3

NEWBORN SCREENING FOR HUMAN DISEASES

Alexander's birth was uneventful. His mother, Celeste, had no complications. The next day, she was up and ready to go home from the hospital. "I couldn't believe how great I felt," she said. But their hospital discharge did not go as expected. Just when the family reached the hospital exit, a frantic nurse came running toward them. Baby Alexander had not yet had his newborn screening test, and he could not go home until it was performed. Celeste wasn't worried about the results of this standard blood test because her first child had also had this test. She and her family went back to the nursery and watched the nurse prick Alexander's heel for drops of blood, which the nurse then put onto a filter paper card. The blood samples would travel to the state's newborn screening lab, which would test them for rare heritable disorders. After the heel prick, Celeste gathered her baby. "Then we left, without giving it another thought."

Nine days later, Celeste was home with both of her sons when her pediatrician called. He asked if Alexander had been fussy. Celeste hadn't noticed anything unusual and told the doctor she thought her baby seemed perfect. Then the doctor said something unexpected. He told her that Alexander's newborn screening test for phenylketonuria (PKU) came back positive. PKU is an inherited disorder that increases the level of an amino acid called phenylalanine (Phe, pronounced "fee") in the blood. PKU is caused by a defect in the *PAH* gene. This gene normally helps make phenylalanine hydroxylase, an enzyme that converts Phe to another amino acid, tyrosine. Cells use tyrosine to make hormones that transmit signals in the brain (neurotransmitters), and to make a pigment called melanin, which gives hair and skin their color. Without treatment, babies with PKU don't develop normally. They have intellectual disabilities and seizures. In the United States, PKU affects about one in every twelve thousand newborns.

Alexander had to have another blood test to confirm his PKU diagnosis. If his second test were positive, he would need to start a special baby formula that is phenylalanine-free. And he would live on a low-protein diet to help manage his medical condition. Celeste became afraid for her child's health and worried about how the condition might affect his quality of life. Despite her distress, Celeste didn't wait for the second test before taking action. When the metabolic nutritionist from a genetics clinic called her, Celeste asked if she could start Alexander on the special formula. He began his new diet the next day.

Alexander was twelve days old when the second test confirmed his PKU diagnosis. His family took him to see a geneticist who explained the disorder and outlined Alexander's treatment plan. The genetic counselor at the clinic discussed the inheritance pattern of PKU, and Celeste and her husband asked questions because they had planned to have more children. They wanted to know their chances of having another child with

PKU. The genetic counselor explained that PKU is an autosomal recessive disorder. If both parents are carriers of a mutation in the *PAH* gene, each of their children has a one-in-four chance of having the disorder. If a baby is born having two mutated copies of the *PAH* gene, one from each parent, then the baby develops PKU.

The metabolic nutritionist at the clinic explained the diet that Alexander would need to follow as an infant (a combination of breast milk and phenylalanine-free formula) and when he began to eat solid foods. Because high concentrations of Phe exist in such foods as meat, eggs, cheese, nuts, grains, and legumes, people with PKU typically avoid those foods and eat lower protein foods like vegetables and fruits. Protein, however, is an essential building block of bones, muscles, cartilage, skin, and blood, so everyone needs to consume it. PKU patients continue to drink a phenylalanine-free protein formula, even as adults.

PKU is a lifelong condition that requires continual diet monitoring and blood testing for Phe level management. A Phe level that is too high can disrupt the function of neurotransmitters in the brain, like dopamine and serotonin, and negatively affect mood, memory, attention, and learning. By monitoring blood Phe on a monthly basis, PKU patients can adjust the diet to keep the blood Phe level in a safe and healthy range.

PKU DISCOVERED

Although genetics is relevant in every field of medicine, knowing the gene sequence does not fully explain the problem causing the disease. Doctors must also know the physiology of each disease to understand and predict the biochemical problem and offer appropriate treatment, if available. In PKU patients, for example, the abnormally high concentrations of phenylalanine in the blood cause neurologic problems. Before doctors understood the effects of elevated Phe levels in humans, children born with PKU went undiagnosed. They developed intellectual and developmental disabilities, and many of them were institutionalized.

The introduction of biochemical tests to identify many infantile-onset diseases—known as newborn screening—has dramatically advanced health care. Newborn screening is a public health breakthrough that allows infants like Alexander to be treated for diseases before they become ill. These tests, however, were not available until after the discovery of PKU.

In 1934 a Norwegian doctor trained in chemistry, Asbjørn Følling, made the first observations of PKU after a mother brought her two children to see him. Both her son and daughter seemed healthy at birth, but they did not develop normally. At three years old, her daughter walked with an unusual gait and could not speak. Her son, at four years old, could not walk, speak, or eat or drink on his own. She told the doctor she thought it was strange that both her children had these symptoms. They also gave off a strange odor in their hair, skin, sweat, and urine.

Følling investigated using biochemistry. He carried out a ferric chloride test for both children. He dissolved a urine sample from each child in a solution of water, ethanol, and ferric chloride. He discovered that both children had a high level of phenylpyruvic acid in their urine. When people lack the enzyme phenylalanine hydroxylase, the Phe in protein converts not to tyrosine but to phenylpyruvic acid, a compound that normal individuals rarely have. This condition was also causing the unusual odor they gave off. Følling tested over four hundred other patients with intellectual disability who lived in an institution, and he found eight of them to be affected with PKU. Følling had discovered PKU with a biochemical test, but he still did not know what caused this condition.

For many years after that, doctors used the ferric chloride urine test to diagnose PKU in patients with intellectual disability or with a family history of the disorder. However, testing every newborn baby for PKU seemed impossible at the time. By the 1950s, doctors recognized the connection between eating Phe from protein in foods and PKU disease. That inspired German pediatrician Horst Bickel, who researched inborn errors of metabolism—rare genetic disorders that result in the body not being able to properly metabolize food—to develop the first PKU formula product in 1953. Bickel and his colleagues tested their formula on a toddler with PKU. The child's behavioral symptoms improved when she stayed on her formula. However, her lack of a diagnosis until she was two years old left her permanently intellectually disabled. From this study, doctors understood they had to start PKU patients on a special diet right after birth. To do that, they needed a reliable screening test to identify newborns with PKU *before* they developed symptoms.

RELIABLE NEWBORN SCREENING

In 1959 Robert Guthrie (1916–1995), whose son was born with developmental disabilities and whose niece had PKU, worked to develop a PKU test that would diagnose infants soon after birth. He created a bacterial inhibition test to detect Phe in the blood. This test uses bacterial growth to detect the presence of a substance in a sample. Guthrie knew that beta-2-Thienylalanine, an amino acid, inhibits the growth of the bacteria *Bacillus subtilis*. Then he found that Phe could interrupt that inhibitory effect. So, to test for elevated levels of Phe, Guthrie grew *Bacillus subtilis* in an agar gel. Then he coated the gel with beta-2-Thienylalanine to prevent further bacterial growth. He placed patient blood samples onto a thick paper filter disc and placed the disc onto the agar gel. If the blood sample contained Phe, bacteria would grow around it. This would indicate that the patient had PKU.

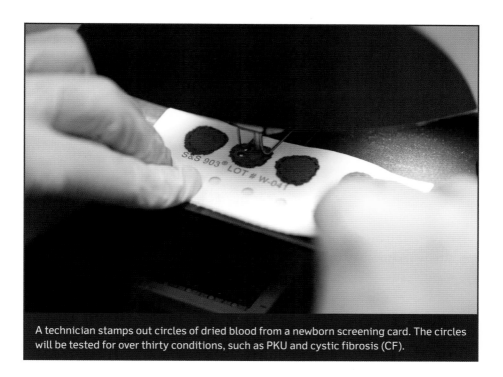

A technician stamps out circles of dried blood from a newborn screening card. The circles will be tested for over thirty conditions, such as PKU and cystic fibrosis (CF).

This testing method required only a small dot of blood from a patient, and it could be used with all newborn infants. Guthrie refined his method and made special cards of thick filter paper, later called Guthrie cards, onto which doctors could collect drops of infant blood. The blood spots dried on the cards. Guthrie then punched 3 mm diameter (0.1-inch) holes in the dried blood spots and placed the sample discs onto the agar gel culture.

After he developed his PKU test, Guthrie lectured throughout the country and abroad to encourage governments to require newborn screening for PKU. Parents of children with PKU also became involved in pushing legislators to require PKU newborn screening in hospitals. In 1963 Massachusetts became the first state to mandate PKU screening using Guthrie cards for all newborns. By 1967 thirty-six states had passed laws requiring

PKU screening in all newborns, and eventually, all fifty states required PKU screening. Each state developed a newborn screening laboratory and hired reporting staff. Thus, the field of newborn screening was born.

Guthrie's work also launched great interest in PKU research and in expanded newborn screening. Other treatable diseases such as sickle cell disease and congenital hypothyroidism were added to the test. But a challenge in newborn screening remained. Each disorder required a specific test on different dried blood spots. And doctors found testing every baby for several diseases to be challenging. In the 1990s, biochemists began using a new technology called tandem mass spectrometry, which is a highly sensitive detection method that can measure hundreds of compounds in a single blood sample. This method, used in all US states and territories, screens for multiple treatable diseases from Guthrie cards.

NEWBORN SCREENING IN THE TWENTY-FIRST CENTURY

Since the development of the PKU test, people have discussed which disorders to include in newborn screening. In 2002 the American College of Medical Genetics (ACMG) developed screening guidelines. At that time, some states screened for only four conditions whereas others screened for as many as fifty. The ACMG looked at many different disorders and placed twenty-nine of them on their Recommended Uniform Screening Panel (RUSP). Among these conditions are such metabolic disorders as maple syrup urine disease, the lung condition cystic fibrosis, and the immunology disorder severe combined immunodeficiency (SCID). A hearing test to detect congenital (inherited) hearing loss, and a pulse oximetry test to detect critical congenital heart disease are also part of newborn screening.

The ACMG also came up with three minimum criteria for new candidate conditions and diseases to be considered for the RUSP:

- The condition can be detected 24 to 48 hours after birth, when it cannot usually be detected by a doctor's exam.
- It has a test that is specific and sensitive for the condition.
- Its early detection, timely intervention, and effective treatment offer proven benefit.

In the United States, the Advisory Committee on Heritable Disorders in Newborns and Children holds regular meetings at which people can make a case for introducing new tests. These meetings result in formal reviews for each condition before the RUSP will add them. Each state's public health department decides which disorders from the RUSP to include on its newborn screening panel. Usually states eventually adopt all the conditions on the RUSP for screening. Newborn screening programs immediately report babies whose results are out of range to the baby's primary care physician. These infants will receive diagnostic testing and, if needed, follow-up care. Although each condition itself is rare, about one baby in every three hundred will be diagnosed with a condition detected by newborn screening.

Newborn screening helps families start their babies early on medical treatment, and it also drives the development of new medical therapies for patients with inherited disorders. In turn, the release of new medical therapies has an impact on the selection of conditions on the RUSP. In 2016, for example, scientists developed a drug called SPINRAZA to treat a severe neurologic disease in infants called spinal muscular atrophy. The US Food and Drug Administration (FDA) approved the drug, making it the first effective treatment for spinal muscular atrophy.

With SPINRAZA's approval, the RUSP added newborn screening for spinal muscular atrophy in 2018.

Most countries with mature health-care systems have newborn screening programs similar to that of the United States, but many smaller and less industrialized countries do not. These countries may lack the metabolic therapies and specialized medical team members to treat babies with these conditions. In 1998 the World Health Organization recommended that newborn screening be mandatory and free, but this has not resulted in universal screening programs. Some of these countries are trying to develop mature newborn screening programs, but these take years to put in place.

TREATING PKU

When Celeste first learned about Alexander's diagnosis, she was confused and worried. She went on the internet to read about PKU, which quickly scared her into thinking that her baby was going to be intellectually disabled or that he would die. Alexander's medical team at the genetics center became the family's lifeline as Celeste and her husband learned how to care for a child with PKU. They met another family with a child who had PKU who helped them find resources. And they learned how to read food labels and find out the Phe content of everything that Alexander would eat. PKU patients can also use such smartphone apps as myPKU and AccuGo, which help families calculate Phe levels in foods and track daily Phe intake. And they can explore PKU cooking and shopping websites for recipes and PKU food products.

Since Alexander's birth, research has advanced PKU medical treatment. In 2007 BioMarin Pharmaceutical, in collaboration with Asubio Pharma, developed and obtained FDA approval for a prescription medicine called KUVAN (sapropterin dihydrochoride) that can help lower the blood Phe levels in some PKU patients.

Kevin Alexander is a PKU patient and advocate who has a YouTube channel and a podcast dedicated to educating others about PKU. You can watch his videos at https://www.youtube.com/user/creativecontrolfilms/.

This medicine is a pharmaceutical version of the chemical tetrahydrobiopterin (BH4), which helps the defective *PAH* enzyme in PKU patients break down phenylalanine. Taking this medicine helps 40 to 50 percent of all PKU patients tolerate more Phe from their foods.

Alexander was lucky to respond well to KUVAN, and he could safely increase his dietary protein allowance. Of his new treatment, thirteen-year-old Alexander said, "Nowadays, PKU is much easier to handle. . . . I used to only be able to eat 8 grams of protein a day, but KUVAN threw that through the roof, and now I can eat up to something like 19.3 [grams]. That allows me to switch from LP (low-protein) pasta to gluten free pasta and eat more in general." Being able to eat more is a big plus for Alexander, who has become a competitive swimmer.

PATIENT RESPONSES

"It can be really tough as a teenager living with PKU, another metabolic disorder, or any medical condition in which you are noticeably different than others your age. It certainly was for me, and I think the hardest part wasn't just the medical diet—it was a perpetual sense of loneliness. I grew up in Shreveport, Louisiana, and I didn't know anyone else affected by PKU. I felt like I didn't really have any peers because no one else I knew understood life with PKU. But things changed for me as an adult when I joined social media sites. I discovered an online community that is extremely supportive, and I've since been able to meet some of those people in person in my trips across the world advocating for PKU awareness. In a perfect world, it would be nice to live in the same city as others with the condition. For those who live in smaller to medium sized cities, or rural areas, that isn't possible. But at the very least, I have discovered that being able to interact with other people online has made my own experience of living with PKU a little bit easier, because I no longer feel alone in my journey."

—Kevin Alexander, videographer, PKU patient

"What is PKU, you ask? I would say PKU is part of who I am. It means my liver cannot process protein. Instead, it breaks it down into a toxin. So, after eating like anyone else (besides anyone else with PKU), over time, my brain would be damaged for eternity. So, I eat a low protein diet, and I love it. I get to do so much more, experience so much more, even though my food choices are far fewer. So overall, I LOVE PKU!"

—Alexander, middle-school student, PKU patient

"Living with PKU has presented its challenges along the way. We have learned so much, met so many wonderful people, and know that this has helped Allen develop into a strong, independent man. Going to PKU conferences all over the country as well as being part of support groups has been a huge help for me in knowing how to best care for Allen. Despite PKU, our family has lived a normal life. We never let it keep us from family vacations or anything else other families do. We are forever thankful for newborn screening. Without it, Allen would be living a very different life."

—Renee, educator and mother of a PKU patient

In 2018 BioMarin took PKU treatment even further when it received FDA approval for a new drug called PALYNZIQ, the first FDA-approved enzyme substitution therapy, to deal with the underlying cause of PKU. PALYNZIQ is an injectable enzyme that reduces blood Phe levels in adult patients whose symptoms don't respond well to other medical and dietary treatments. This revolutionary treatment could help many PKU patients live more easily with their disorder.

Allen, a nineteen-year-old PKU patient, was the first person in his state to be prescribed PALYNZIQ in October 2018. His medical team members taught him how to inject himself with his new medicine. "The first injection was hard," Allen said, "because I've never given myself a shot before so I wasn't sure how it would feel. I recently did my second injection at home. It was so much easier and I was able to do it without hesitation. Even though I haven't experienced any benefits from the injection yet, I am excited for what's to come. I'm looking forward to being able to eat more." When asked what he would like others to know about living with PKU, Allen said, "Living with PKU is not so bad. I don't see myself as different. Now that I am working, most people do not even know what I have. I think I would still be the same person I am now even if I didn't have PKU."

Over twelve thousand children born each year in the United States benefit from an early diagnosis of a treatable condition on the RUSP. Having saved countless lives, newborn screening is a highly important and effective public health innovation.

CHAPTER 4
READING THE GENOME

Hospitals and clinics currently use genetic tests for a wide variety of diagnostic and therapeutic purposes. Doctors offer testing to parents if a genetic condition runs in the family or if they come from an ethnic group in which a genetic disorder is more likely to occur. For example, the genetic mutations that cause Tay-Sachs disease, a severe neurodegenerative condition, occur more frequently in people of Ashkenazi Jewish heritage from eastern and central Europe. And beta-thalassemia, a disease involving hemoglobin deficiency, occurs more commonly in people of Mediterranean, North African, Middle Eastern, or Central or Southeast Asian heritage.

The use of DNA testing as one tool to diagnose complex diseases would not have been possible without decades of research and experimentation. Wilkins, Watson, Franklin, and Crick discovered the chemical structure of DNA, but their achievement did not decode the information within human genes. Breaking the code of DNA—the sequence of its base pairs—was the key to understanding how DNA was essential to biology and DNA replication.

Before geneticists could use genetic testing to help patients, they had to understand how the sequence of base pairs leads to the biological effects of DNA. According to the National Human Genome Research Institute, "The sequence tells scientists the kind of genetic information that is carried in a particular DNA segment. For example, scientists can use sequence information to determine which stretches of DNA contain genes and which stretches carry regulatory instructions, turning genes on or off."

Geneticists also needed to understand the exact sequence that makes up each particular gene to figure out where one gene ends and the next one begins. They also had to comprehend what effect each gene has on biological functions. After unraveling these scientific mysteries, geneticists could then look for pathogenic mutations that might interfere with normal biological functions and use that information to make a medical diagnosis.

Guthrie's blood sample method of newborn screening for PKU worked fine for diagnosing a PKU patient, but it did not

HOW DOES DNA CODE FOR PROTEIN SYNTHESIS?

DNA codes for protein in two steps. First, enzymes read information in a DNA molecule and transcribe it into an intermediary molecule called messenger ribonucleic acid (mRNA). This is called *transcription*. Then mRNA is translated into a strand of amino acids that makes up a functional protein (*translation*). There are twenty-two different amino acids. Each protein is created by a different combination of amino acids and has a specific function in the body. Hemoglobin, for example, is a protein that carries oxygen in the blood. Collagen is a structural protein in bones, tendons, ligaments, and skin. Antibodies are proteins that protect the body from harmful bacteria and viruses.

WHAT IS DNA?

Human cells contain hereditary material called deoxyribonucleic acid (DNA). DNA is made up of four chemical units, called nucleotide bases: adenine, thymine, guanine, and cytosine—or A, T, G, and C, respectively. DNA is a two-stranded molecule, with a double-helix shape, and in humans it consists of about three billion base pairs per cell. The two strands that form the backbone of the DNA structure are made of sugars and phosphates. The nucleotide bases connecting the two strands make specific pairs: adenine (A) pairs with thymine (T), and cytosine (C) pairs with guanine (G). The order, or sequence, of these bases determines the instructions of the genome, which is the organism's complete set of DNA, including all of its genes. These genes are compacted into chromosomes, threadlike structures found in the cell nucleus. Humans inherit twenty-three pairs of chromosomes, one set from each parent. One of these pairs are sex chromosomes. The other twenty-two pairs are autosomes.

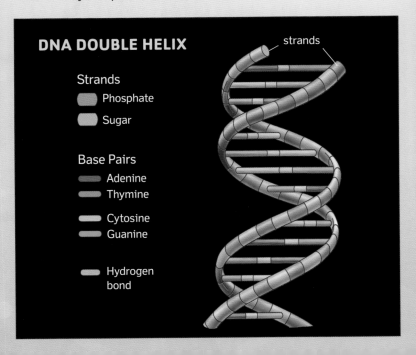

DNA DOUBLE HELIX

strands

Strands

- Phosphate
- Sugar

Base Pairs

- Adenine
- Thymine

- Cytosine
- Guanine

- Hydrogen bond

help identify DNA mutation carriers—people who were at risk for passing their mutations in the *PAH* gene to their offspring. Doctors suspected many diseases were genetically inherited, but until they could read the genome, they could not understand each gene's specific function, nor which mutations caused disease. A method was needed to sequence DNA and look for normal and abnormal sequences. That method was Sanger sequencing.

SANGER SEQUENCING

In 1961 Marshall Nirenberg (1927–2010) at the National Institutes of Health and Har Gobind Khorana (1922–2011) at the University of Wisconsin–Madison cracked what is often called "the code for life." They discovered how the nucleotides of DNA are transcribed into an RNA strand that the cell "reads" in blocks of three nucleotides, called codons. Each codon determines the correct amino acid to use during protein synthesis. Nirenberg and Khorana's work to decipher the genetic code led the way for other scientists to devise techniques for sequencing DNA, or identifying the order of the nucleotide bases. Once researchers could read the base pair sequence in groups of three nucleotides, then they could understand the amino acid sequence of the protein.

In 1977 British biochemist Frederick Sanger (1918–2013) at the University of Cambridge, England, was one of the first people to develop a method for sequencing DNA. Sanger understood that DNA has to replicate before cells can divide. He also realized that before DNA replicates, the base pairs of the double helix "unzip," resulting in two strands of complementary nucleotides. Each strand is called a template. An enzyme called DNA polymerase creates a complementary strand from one end to the other on each template. Sanger developed a method to visualize this replication by making nucleotides radioactive so that they could be seen on X-ray film. Here's how Sanger did it:

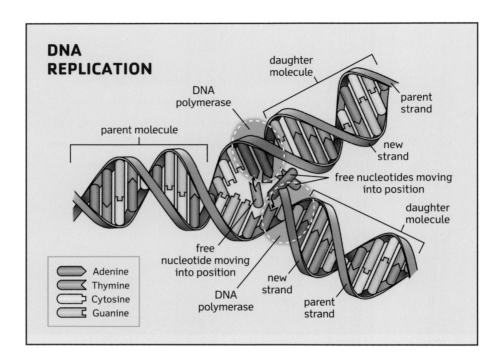

DNA REPLICATION

daughter molecule

DNA polymerase

parent strand

parent molecule

new strand

free nucleotides moving into position

daughter molecule

free nucleotide moving into position

new strand

DNA polymerase

parent strand

Adenine
Thymine
Cytosine
Guanine

Sanger made four mixtures in separate test tubes for his experiment. Each mixture contained the same DNA template, DNA polymerase, and all four nucleotide bases—adenine (A), thymine (T), cytosine (C), and guanine (G). Next, Sanger added a radioactive version of each nucleotide to each tube— radioactive adenine to one tube, radioactive thymine to the next, and so on. The replication incorporated these radioactive nucleotides into the new DNA strand but prevented the DNA from continuing to replicate, or extend, further. That is why each radioactive nucleotide is also called a *terminal base*. During Sanger's experiment, the nucleotide bases combined to create a complementary strand of the template, nucleotide by nucleotide, until a terminal base stopped the replication. This happened over and over again, with strands of different lengths being created— sometimes the radioactive nucleotide would join the strand early, stopping the replication when the strand was still very short, and other times it would join later, creating a longer strand. When the process was completed, each tube contained a mixture of every length extension of the DNA template terminated by the nucleotide in that tube. For example, in the tube with radioactive thymine, all possible fragments ending with a T were present. This method was called *chain-termination sequencing*, or more commonly, Sanger sequencing.

The next step was to take images of these strands on X-ray film. Sanger used gel electrophoresis to separate the DNA strands of different lengths in each of the four tubes. He used a gel with four channels, each filled at the top with one of the four DNA mixtures. Electrophoresis uses an electrical current, which makes the DNA fragments migrate through the gel according to their size. The shorter fragments travel faster, and the larger fragments move more slowly. After running the electrophoresis for a certain length of time, Sanger then put an X-ray film next to the gel. Only the radioactive nucleotides at the end of each DNA fragment could be seen on the X-ray film. Sanger had created a sort of ladder of all the fragments that terminated with a radioactive nucleotide. By reading up from the bottom, the complementary sequence to the template could be read. With this process, Sanger sequenced the genome of a virus that had 5,386 nucleotides. (For comparison, the human genome has over 3 billion nucleotide pairs.)

A huge breakthrough, Sanger sequencing became the standard method for genetic sequencing from the 1970s to the mid-2000s. It allowed the creation of DNA sequences from human tissue—typically from white blood cells—for the first time. Scientists in many fields beyond genetics benefited from Sanger sequencing. Zoologists began sequencing animal DNA and refined their ideas about species evolution. Archaeologists too began to use DNA sequencing to advance their analysis of human, animal, and plant specimens. This tool gave archaeologists genetic evidence for ancient human migrations. Crime labs also

SANGER SEQUENCING: AN EXAMPLE

To understand better how Sanger sequencing works, take a look at this example.

The template sequence of CAGATCGA has a complementary strand with the sequence GTCTAGCT. After the extension reaction based on the template, you would have the following chains (where the asterisk indicates a radioactive nucleotide):

chain 1:	G*
chain 2:	GT*
chain 3:	GTC*
chain 4:	GTCT*
chain 5:	GTCTA*
chain 6:	GTCTAG*
chain 7:	GTCTAGC*
chain 8:	GTCTAGCT*

In the tube containing G*, chains would terminate the growing strand wherever there was G*, as in chains 1 and 6. In the T* tube, there would be chains 2, 4, and 8. In the C* tube, there are chains 3 and 7. And in the A* tube, there is chain 5. After DNA replication and chain termination, gel electrophoresis separates the strands by size. The gel is then put next to an X-ray film. When the film is developed, only the radioactive nucleotides can be seen, appearing as spots on the film. When read up from the bottom, the spots reveal the sequence GTCTAGCT. From this complementary sequence, the template sequence can be inferred.

G	T	C	A	
	—			Chain 8 ends in T*.
		—		Chain 7 ends in C*.
—				Chain 6 ends in G*.
			—	Chain 5 ends in A*.
	—			Chain 4 ends in T*.
		—		Chain 3 ends in C*.
	—			Chain 2 ends in T*.
—				Chain 1 ends in G*.

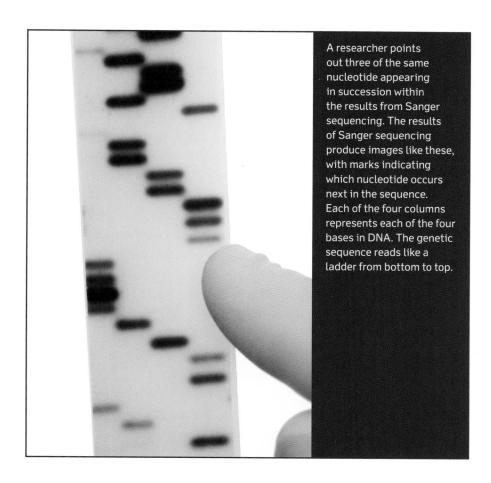

A researcher points out three of the same nucleotide appearing in succession within the results from Sanger sequencing. The results of Sanger sequencing produce images like these, with marks indicating which nucleotide occurs next in the sequence. Each of the four columns represents each of the four bases in DNA. The genetic sequence reads like a ladder from bottom to top.

began to use DNA sequencing to prove paternity in rape cases. And forensic teams started collecting DNA samples left at crime scenes to match them with the DNA of a criminal suspect.

GENETIC MAPPING

One of the most useful applications of genetic sequencing is in the diagnosis of inherited diseases, such as cystic fibrosis. CF is one of the most common inherited diseases, and patients are often hospitalized because of their illness. Everyone carries two copies of the cystic fibrosis transmembrane conductance regulator (CFTR) gene, but in people with CF, both copies of their CFTR gene are mutated, disrupting the normal production or functioning of the

CFTR protein found in the cells of the lungs and other parts of the body. This protein helps regulate the flow of salt and fluids in and out of the cells in different parts of the body. Without it, patients experience a build-up of thick, sticky mucus and get infections in the lungs, pancreas, and other organs.

But researchers didn't always know about the *CFTR* gene, let alone how to properly treat CF. In the 1980s, the life expectancy for a CF patient in the United States was only twelve years. The disease mutations are more commonly found in descendants of northern Europeans, but CF is panethnic, or seen in all populations. Doctors needed to identify the mutations that caused CF so they could diagnose patients at an early age, before they became ill. By knowing the mutations, they could also identify carriers of the disease who planned to have children and offer them genetic counseling before pregnancy.

In 1989 a collaborative group of researchers from the Hospital for Sick Children in Toronto, Canada, led by Lap-Chee Tsui, and from the University of Michigan, led by Francis Collins, used genetic mapping to discover the gene that causes cystic fibrosis. Mapping can tell researchers which chromosome contains the gene and where on the chromosome the gene is. The National Human Genome Research Institute explains genetic mapping in this way:

> To produce a genetic map, researchers collect blood or tissue samples from members of families in which a certain disease or trait is prevalent. Using various laboratory techniques, the scientists isolate DNA from these samples and examine it for unique patterns that are seen only in family members who have the disease or trait. These characteristic patterns in the chemical bases that make up DNA are referred to as

markers. DNA markers don't, by themselves, identify the gene responsible for the disease or trait, but they can tell researchers roughly where the gene is on the chromosome.

By studying families of CF patients, the collaborative team finally found a common mutation in a genetic sequence that they could prove was the gene associated with cystic fibrosis. After discovering the *CFTR* gene, they were able to find the various mutations that caused CF. To date, geneticists have found over seventeen hundred different mutations that cause this disease, and these mutations affect patients in different ways. This is genotype-phenotype correlation. It can help to predict the symptoms affected individuals will experience by identifying their mutations. And that, in turn, helps doctors figure out the best treatments for their patients. As Christine Bear, codirector of the CF Center at the Hospital for Sick Children, said, "After [the gene's] discovery, we were able to study and understand how the protein made by the *CFTR* gene worked and what happened when it didn't. . . . Once we figured this out, therapy that targeted defects caused by CF gene mutations could begin."

Genetic sequencing of the *CFTR* gene can also identify people who carry a single copy of the CF mutation. This does not cause disease in them because they have another normal copy. Doctors can counsel CF carriers and explain their risks of passing their gene mutation on to their child. If both parents are carriers, in each pregnancy, there is a 25 percent chance that both parents will pass on their mutated gene and that the child will have CF.

In 2005 only five states in the US required that CF be included on the list of mandatory screening conditions. By 2009 all fifty states mandated newborn screening for CF because doctors had shown that early diagnosis and treatment of CF could have a dramatic impact on the health of children born with the condition.

HUMAN GENOME PROJECT

After seeing the successes of genetic sequencing, geneticists in many countries talked about sequencing the entire human genome. Some thought this would advance treatment for inherited diseases, but others believed that sequencing the entire genome could be a waste of time and money. At that time, no one knew exactly how much of our DNA coded for proteins or how much of it held noncoding sequences with unknown functions. Some wondered why we would analyze hundreds of thousands of sequences that did not code for proteins. Others pointed out that we might discover what vital functions these sequences have.

Despite the debate, the push for genetic sequencing continued when the US government became involved. During the 1980s, the US Department of Energy (DOE) wanted to know the effects of radiation on the human genome. Meanwhile, the NIH wanted to develop genetic medicine. So, in 1988, the US Congress funded the Human Genome Project to map human and other genomes—including those of fruit flies and mice—and to study the ethical, legal, and social issues (ELSI) of DNA research. The ELSI Research Program funds and manages studies and supports workshops, research groups, and policy conferences about genetic and genomic research, health care, and broader legal, policy, and societal issues.

In 1990 the DOE and NIH published a research plan for the first five years of what they expected to be a fifteen-year project. The plan would be carried out as a unique collaboration between many sequencing laboratories, coordinated by the NIH. In 2001 the Human Genome Project's international consortium published its first draft and analysis of the human genome sequence in the journal *Nature*. One day later, biochemist and geneticist Craig Venter, who had left the NIH and helped start private company Celera Genomics to sequence the human genome using a

THE ETHICAL, LEGAL, AND SOCIAL IMPLICATIONS (ELSI) RESEARCH PROGRAM

Researchers who worked on the Human Genome Project understood that important questions would arise as to who should have access to personal genomic information. Should insurance companies know what's in a patient's genome? Should family members? People wanted to know where genomic research was headed and what the ethical, legal, and social implications of the work were. ELSI, an integral part of the Human Genome Project, was established in 1990 to address these issues, identify problems, and find solutions *before* scientific information was integrated into the health-care system.

ELSI has held numerous conferences with a goal of developing consensus and guidelines around the uses of genetic testing. It also operates to establish standards for collecting consent for genetic testing and for results reporting. ELSI provides funding for research focused on ethical, legal, and social issues in genetics and genomics. It also helps to develop legislation to prevent discrimination in health-care insurance based on genetic test results.

Federal legislation to protect against discrimination based on genetic information was passed in May 2008. The Genetics Information Nondiscrimination Act, signed by President George W. Bush, protects individuals from discrimination based on genetic information in health insurance and employment. (To learn more about ELSI, check out the Further Information section.)

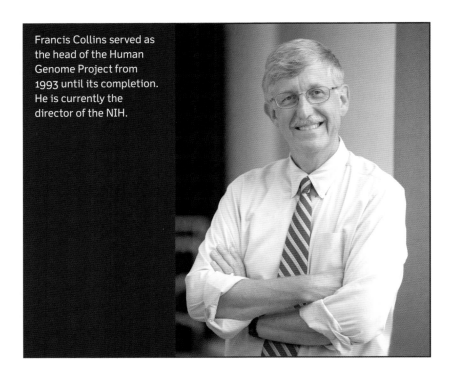

Francis Collins served as the head of the Human Genome Project from 1993 until its completion. He is currently the director of the NIH.

different sequencing method, also published his project's results on the human genome in the journal *Science*. Two years later, the Human Genome Project announced that its project was complete.

"It's a history book—a narrative of the journey of our species through time," said Francis Collins, former director of the National Human Genome Research Institute of NIH. "It's a shop manual, with an incredibly detailed blueprint for building every human cell. And it's a transformative textbook of medicine, with insights that will give health care providers immense new powers to treat, prevent, and cure disease."

The Human Genome Project gave the world invaluable information. We know, for example, that the human genome contains 3.2 billion base pairs that encode for about twenty thousand to twenty-five thousand genes. Despite those large numbers, all humans are 99.9 percent identical in genetic makeup. The remaining 0.1 percent accounts for our differences in traits—such as hair, eye, and skin color—and it has an effect on the diseases we may develop. The project also advanced the research of genetic diseases by providing the scientific community with DNA sequences they could study to help with the diagnosis and treatment of patients with heritable diseases.

Another vital piece of information that came from the Human Genome project is that genes are only a small part of the genome, between 1 and 2 percent. One goal of future genetic research is to understand more about the remaining 98 to 99 percent of the genome that does not code for protein, which scientists call noncoding DNA. Recent research has shown that sequences that control the expression of genes make up some of the noncoding DNA. The amount of protein a gene makes, or whether it can make any protein at all, is controlled by gene expression. To figure out the purpose of our noncoding DNA, NIH created a follow-up initiative to the Human Genome Project: ENCODE (Encyclopedia of DNA Elements). ENCODE's work is ongoing, with some thirty research groups located throughout the United States.

The Human Genome Project, which used Sanger sequencing, took ten years, costing billions of dollars to sequence the first genome. After the project's completion, researchers realized that updated sequencing techniques and computer-based analytical methods were needed to make DNA-based sequencing practical for medical diagnosis and therapy. They also realized that the sequence genome, or reference genome, which came from samples from a small group of volunteers, was too limited for the world's genetically diverse population. A genetic study of people of African descent has shown that the reference genome is missing up to three hundred million nucleotides found in their genomes. As scientists learn more about both gene function and expression, and genetic diversity, they will better understand how our genome affects our health.

CHAPTER 5
NEXT-GENERATION SEQUENCING

Eight-year-old Frances is used to hospitals. She and her twin brother were born seven weeks before their expected delivery date. Frances weighed only 2.5 pounds (1.1 kg) at birth, and she didn't eat and grow as well as her brother. (Most newborns weigh between 5.5 and 8.7 pounds, or 2.5 and 4 kg.) She also had neurological abnormalities and mild facial dysmorphisms (abnormalities). Frances had to stay in the hospital for two months and finally came home wearing a heart monitor and needing supplemental oxygen. As a baby and toddler, Frances continued to have trouble feeding. She also needed brain surgery for hydrocephalus (excess fluid in the ventricles of the brain) and oral surgery to remove the extra tissue that pulled the tip of her tongue to the bottom of her mouth (a condition called tongue-tie). As she grew, Frances still could not swallow solid food and relied on liquid nutrition.

Frances also could not speak for the first five years of her life, but she understood spoken language. She used sign language and an augmented communication device (an iPad with TouchChat software) with her family and at school. Then, at five years old, she began to use her voice to communicate. In three years, she learned so much spoken language that her mother, Louise, says she sounds like a normal eight-year-old with a speech impediment.

Despite her medical challenges, Frances has what Louise calls "a sunny personality." She is sensitive and kind to her brother and friends at school. She is resilient and hardworking, and her teachers and special therapists adore her. Frances also loves sports. She's on a swim team, zooms around on roller skates, and plays lacrosse. When Frances has to interrupt her life to go to another doctor's appointment or have another surgery, she doesn't complain.

Her parents live by the idea that they can "assume competence" in their daughter, which means they believe she can meet her goals and live a fulfilling life. They always wondered, however, what caused Frances's condition. Was it due to her being born prematurely? Or did she have a genetic condition that her twin brother did not have?

Doctors suspected Frances might have Prader-Willi syndrome, a genetic disorder that affects cognitive function, metabolism, muscle tone, metabolism, and growth. This disorder is caused by a chromosomal deletion. If not Prader-Willi, doctors thought Frances could have fragile X syndrome, a genetic condition that causes learning disabilities and cognitive impairment, or Worster Drought syndrome, a condition that affects the muscles of the mouth and throat. They ran tests for all of these. Louise didn't understand why doctors were trying to fit her daughter's condition into all these diagnoses, none of which matched up completely with Frances's symptoms. "Nothing felt quite right, and it all felt like putting a round peg in a square hole," Louise said. But that's how

CHROMOSOMAL DUPLICATIONS AND DELETIONS

Human chromosomal duplications occur when extra copies of a chromosome region are formed. This leads to extra copies of genes found in that part of the chromosome. Chromosomal deletions occur when DNA sequences are lost, leading to missing genes. Extra genes can make extra proteins, while missing genes fail to make necessary proteins, either of which affects the phenotype of the person. Both duplications and deletions can happen during cell division when chromosomes align, and these changes can involve hundreds of thousands of base pairs.

Charcot-Marie-Tooth disease type 1 is a disorder caused by a chromosomal duplication that leads to nerve damage and loss of normal function of the limbs. It is caused by a duplication of a gene on chromosome 17 that carries instructions for producing the protective coating of nerves. Wolf-Hirschhorn syndrome is caused by a deletion of the short arm of chromosome 4. This disorder results in facial dysmorphisms, intellectual disability, delayed development, and seizures. Geneticists have described many other disorders that stem from chromosomal duplications and deletions.

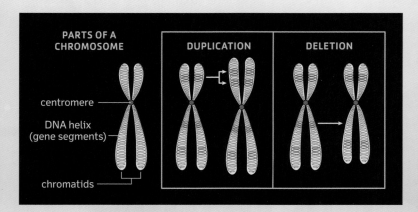

PARTS OF A CHROMOSOME

centromere

DNA helix (gene segments)

chromatids

DUPLICATION

DELETION

doctors often rule out certain disorders and pinpoint a diagnosis. They test for disorders they already understand to make sure what they're seeing in a patient like Frances is indeed something new to them. Incomplete information about genetic medicine and brain development can limit accurate diagnosis and treatment. Some disorders are so rare that doctors are still learning about them.

MASSIVELY PARALLEL SEQUENCING

One of the limitations of the Human Genome Project was that Sanger sequencing was too slow and expensive to move the field of genetics into clinical medicine. The Human Genome Project was a collaborative effort of over a thousand geneticists who, after ten years, were able to complete a single human genome. That genome sequence of 3.2 billion base pairs cost $2.7 billion to produce. If genetic sequencing was to become a significant part of health care and science, it had to be quicker and less expensive.

In the early twenty-first century, genetic scientists developed new methods that allowed sequencing of many thousands of DNA fragments simultaneously. These methods were collectively called massively parallel sequencing, or next-generation sequencing (NGS), and no longer needed the radioactive nucleotides involved in Sanger sequencing. Besides being roughly a thousand times more efficient, NGS does not require gels or radiographic films.

Next-generation sequencing takes a patient's DNA sample and breaks it into many millions of fragments. Unlike in Sanger sequencing, each of the DNA fragments is sequenced multiple times. This redundant sequencing of the sample is called read depth. Every patient sample must have an adequate read depth to be considered accurate, and so researchers usually sequence it between twenty and two hundred times. Computers then compare the patient's sample sequence data to a normal

In addition to identifying mutations in humans, researchers use next-generation sequencing to examine the genomes of bacteria that cause foodborne illness. Understanding the genetic makeup of these disease-causing bacteria can help scientists identify ways to protect people from ingesting them.

reference DNA sequence, one that doesn't have any mutations, and analyze it for discrepancies. These discrepancies are then categorized into groups:

- Pathogenic. There is a risk of developing a disorder or a disease.
- Likely pathogenic. There is strong evidence that the variant is pathogenic.
- Likely benign. There is strong evidence that the variant is benign.
- Benign. The variant is not associated with a risk for disease.
- Variants of uncertain significance. There is not enough evidence to classify the variant, or evidence is conflicting about whether it is pathogenic or benign.

USING SEQUENCING METHODS IN HEALTH CARE

The causes of genetic diseases can vary drastically from person to person, so doctors cannot always determine which gene mutation has caused a patient's problem. Next-generation sequencing helps doctors overcome this issue because it can sequence hundreds of millions of base pairs from a single drop of blood or saliva. Doctors can use three categories of diagnostic NGS tests to look for pathogenic variants in patients: gene panels, whole exome sequencing, and whole genome sequencing.

GENE PANELS

A gene panel is a type of NGS test that groups together otherwise physically disconnected genes. Each gene is known to cause similar symptoms. For example, doctors may order an epilepsy panel of over one hundred genes to look for a genetic cause in children with a seizure disorder. The testing laboratory will sequence only those genes on the panel and report any variants found. Gene panels focus on all the known genes for a clinical phenotype, and they give doctors the best possibility of finding a genetic cause for a disease. Gene panels are frequently updated as new gene mutations are discovered.

WHOLE EXOME SEQUENCING

A more expanded test than a gene panel test is the whole exome sequence (WES). This test sequences the exome, the entire coding region in the genome, which contains the exons. WES is typically ordered when the patient's clinical symptoms do not resemble those of a known disorder and a gene panel cannot be used. One limitation of this method, however, is that it does not offer any information about the noncoding DNA.

WHOLE GENOME SEQUENCING

Whole genome sequencing (WGS) is even more extensive than whole exome testing. It is not limited to the exome but offers sequence analysis of all 3.2 billion base pairs in a patient. One benefit of WGS is that it detects deletions and duplications of entire parts of chromosomes, which can cause disease, in contrast to whole exome testing and gene panels, which cannot detect such deletions and duplications. Another important advantage of WGS is that the entire genome is sequenced including introns and other noncoding regions. Geneticists used to believe that introns were unimportant for disease diagnosis, calling them junk DNA. That view has changed, and scientists are uncovering new ways in which introns affect how genes are expressed. For instance, beta-thalassemia is sometimes caused by a point mutation in an intron that affects the normal protein sequence. Because the point mutation makes an abnormal messenger RNA, people with this problem make too little of one protein in hemoglobin, the oxygen-carrying molecule in red blood cells.

WGS is still very expensive, and often insurance companies won't cover it, so many doctors do not request it. That is changing as the costs for WGS come down. In the future, personal WGS will likely become a standard part of health care.

LIMITATIONS AND BENEFITS OF NEXT-GENERATION SEQUENCING

Next-generation sequencing methods themselves are not foolproof and can introduce rare errors into the sequencing results. So most NGS testing sequences each base pair at least thirty times, and sometimes hundreds of times. Also, DNA samples that contain repeating sequences of base pairs often produce unreliable results. This is a problem because some patients have an amplification (massive replication) of nucleotide repeats. Accurately sequencing such repeats is important for detecting disease. For example, in the *FMR-1* gene, the normal sequence has fewer than fifty-five repeats of the codon CGG. Individuals with fragile X syndrome, a neurologic disorder, have more than two hundred CGG repeats. Because NGS does not reliably sequence base pair repeats, it is not useful for identifying fragile X or other conditions with similar genetic causes. Different techniques are needed to diagnose these conditions.

However, NGS offers doctors the opportunity to detect a patient's genetic predispositions to disease before disease actually occurs. Presymptomatic testing is important in families who have a history of treatable diseases that often have a genetic cause, such as certain forms of cancer or heart disease. If a gene panel test reveals that a patient carries pathogenic variants associated with breast cancer, the patient can increase cancer surveillance through frequent mammograms or have surgery before the disease occurs. Some people choose to have bilateral mastectomies even though they do not have cancer at the time. They do this to protect themselves for the future.

Doctors can also use noninvasive methods to test for genetic abnormalities in a fetus. During a pregnancy, the mother's blood has an extremely small amount of the fetus's DNA in her blood stream. By simply taking the mother's blood and performing NGS testing on the fetal DNA, certain abnormalities can be detected before the child is born.

These are just some of the ways that NGS has improved health care in the past decade. But those benefits are not without complications. Human genetic variation is common and vast. Because of the mass of new data generated with NGS, scientists see many variants of uncertain significance. Doctors don't know what each variation could mean for each person. They are unsure what to tell patients and families when NGS identifies a variant that no one has seen before. In these cases, doctors often say to a patient, "You have a genetic sequence variant, but we don't know what it means." For some patients, this uncertainty causes anxiety. But until geneticists discover the effects of all possible variants, this problem of uncertainty will remain.

To make NGS tests more useful in clinical care, doctors need a better understanding of the role of each individual sequence variant and the significance of carrying multiple

ALL OF US RESEARCH PROGRAM

The All of Us Research Program, started in 2018, is a national initiative in the United States to gather data from one million or more participants to further research and advance precision medicine. The goal of precision medicine is to help people understand the best way to stay healthy. Anyone over the age of eighteen who is living in the United States can join the All of Us program at no cost. After giving their consent, participants will be asked about their health and lifestyle. They may also be asked to give a urine sample and a blood sample for inclusion in a national database of genetic information that has been stripped of personal information. The blood sample could be used for genotyping and whole genome sequencing. The purpose of this database is to help researchers, including citizen scientists, to conduct health studies and make new medical discoveries from data.

The program will also return the genetic data to its participants, which gives them ownership of their own data. They can also stop participating at any time. The program collaborators hope to interest people from diverse backgrounds and lifestyles so that medical studies can be inclusive genetic variations. Acquiring this understanding will take decades of scientific collaboration. New genetic diseases are being discovered and characterized each year. Many clinical and genetic databases catalog clinical phenotypes and variants that are seen in patients. ClinVar and the Online Mendelian Inheritance in Man (OMIM) are two examples of such databases. Clinicians often search these databases for answers to clinical genetic problems. It will take many years before scientists fully understand how genetic variants cause disease.

and expansive. Such diversity helps medical researchers understand how health conditions affect different people in different ways. "Diversity is a hallmark of this effort. We strive for diversity of people and also diversity of data types, so researchers can understand the many factors that influence health and health outcomes for each of us," said Eric Dishman, director of the All of Us Research Program.

The All of Us Research Program collaborators believe it may take five years to gather one million participants. Researchers and participants alike ask how the information should be shared so that data is both protected and useful for different research groups. With regard to access, the program's deputy director, Stephanie Devaney, states, "We are not limited to just folks who work at a certain institution or even who live in the United States. We will be open for foreign researchers, and we will be open for folks into the private sector and the government and academia and even ultimately citizen scientists or community scientists."

Visit https://allofus.nih.gov/about/participation for more information.

DIAGNOSIS BY WHOLE EXOME TESTING

When Frances had specific genetic testing by gene panels, the results came back normal. With the gene-testing methods available at the time, doctors could not figure out a genetic cause of Frances's medical condition. They could still treat her symptoms but had to do this without making a firm diagnosis. In 2018, however, when Frances was eight, whole exome testing became far more affordable. Her doctor ordered this test. This time, the results showed that Frances has a single copy of a pathogenic variant in a newly described gene called *KAT6A*. Researchers have only recently found this autosomal dominant condition in children who had neurologic deficits similar to Frances's. The new diagnosis was key to understanding her health. It explained what was causing Frances's difficulty to swallow and speak, for example. Then Frances's doctors could connect with the genetic scientists who described this disorder.

KAT6A syndrome is a rare genetic neurodevelopmental disorder that affects children in different ways. The disorder is most often caused by de novo mutations. They are not inherited from either parent but rather spontaneously appear in offspring. The syndrome was first described in 2015 in two independent series of patients. The diagnosis in all ten patients was based on whole exome testing and led to the discovery of this new disease. As of August 2019, only two hundred people in the world were known to have it. The syndrome is so rare that few doctors are familiar with it, so it can be misdiagnosed or go undiagnosed. Nobody knows exactly how many other people have the disorder. Common symptoms include speech delays, intellectual disability, feeding problems, and diminished muscle tone. *KAT6A* syndrome can also cause abnormalities of the heart, eyes, and teeth, but affected children may differ in their symptoms.

PATIENT RESPONSES

"While experts in the NICU recognized symptoms in Frances when she was born and ordered multiple genetic tests, both the science and diagnosis didn't exist when Frances was born. If she had been born today, and specialists ordered the whole exome test, we may be able to complement the intense therapy she received with medical treatments that would make her even more able and successful. We feel time has been lost and this will affect her life's outcomes. Availability of geneticists and genetic developments will have significant positive impacts on real people's lives."

—Frances's father, Michael

"When we received the *KAT6A* diagnosis, we were able to work backwards and identify areas of concern that we shared with other *KAT6A* patients. Frances has presented herself differently than others in many ways (as every patient does). But there is a common denominator that we can now identify. I am not sure doctors would ever have concluded *KAT6A* on symptoms alone. Frances also has medical issues not consistent with the syndrome. We are now able to look at those as independent conditions, and treat accordingly."

—Frances's mother, Louise

With the diagnosis, Frances's doctors and parents can follow research on the syndrome. Geneticists have found no cure for *KAT6A* syndrome, but they are studying the different ways it affects patients and sometimes suggesting a formula of carnitine and B vitamins that may be of benefit. Frances's mother, Louise, was informed of a *KAT6A* syndrome patient Facebook group where she can communicate with other parents of children with *KAT6A* mutations. They let one another know about clinical studies and support one another through times of uncertainty and hardship.

Louise takes Frances to see a neurologist who has helped immensely with Frances's care. They also attended an in-patient feeding clinic where Frances learned to eat soft foods like bananas, berries, yogurt, and hummus for the first time. Frances is still exploring new tastes and discovering which foods she likes best.

Louise also consulted a geneticist who she thought was too directive in his recommendations. He told her she should consider sterilization as a way to prevent Frances from having children who might inherit *KAT6A* and then suffer from it. He also told her of the high incidence of rape of people with intellectual disability. Upset by this discussion, Louise soon talked to another geneticist who said that such directive consultations were never a part of his clinic's patient care. Louise's experience is too common in the disability community and highlights the importance of including disabled people and their loved ones in discussions about the ethics and policies of genetic medicine. Louise is fortunate that she can find another geneticist who is respectful and sensitive in this complex situation to help tailor a personalized medicine plan for Frances.

INTEGRATING GENETIC TESTING INTO HEALTH CARE

Through the next several years, as new genetic research comes out, it might be hard for health care to keep up. Many people wonder if one day we will all have a copy of our whole genome sequence results in our medical records. Some are already taking that step on their own by ordering direct-to-consumer whole exome or whole genome testing or by visiting a concierge clinic and paying for genetic testing out of pocket. If we did have these test results in our medical record, our primary care doctor might be able to use them to help prevent or treat our genetic medical conditions.

As geneticists learn more about the human genome and its various mutations, they can begin to offer more specialized care based on their patients' individual genetic testing results. However, not all mutations present in a patient's genome affect their health. Robert C. Green (*left*) is a geneticist who tested positive for a mutation associated with a condition that causes facial deformities, but he does not possess the disorder.

But most physicians know very little about interpreting genetic sequences. So, if they suspect a possible genetic cause for disease, they might refer a patient to a specialist. Currently, however, the number of trained medical geneticists and genetic counselors is desperately low while the demand for their services is growing rapidly. Patients often have to wait many months or travel long distances to have an appointment with a geneticist. Even when they see a specialist and take NGS tests, they are not guaranteed a clear diagnosis or effective treatment,

> 66 Scientists caught up in the excitement of genetics discoveries can forget that life with a disability can be rich and fulfilling. 'Health' is a subjective characterization, most often defined by health professionals, researchers, and the insurance industry, and not by people with disabilities."

—Paul Steven Miller and Rebecca Leah Levine

especially if they, like Frances, are found to have a newly described disorder.

With more information about the effects of the entire genome on health and disease becoming available each year, medical researchers of the future will have to develop more specific and predictive tests to guide patients throughout their lives. These new developments are all part of precision medicine or, as it is more commonly called, personalized medicine.

CHAPTER 6
DIRECT-TO-CONSUMER GENETIC TESTING

In 2007 Lily saw an ad for a direct-to-consumer ancestral DNA test through the Genographic Project of the National Geographic Society. The project studies prehistoric migration patterns of human populations. It was founded in 2005 by geneticist Spencer Wells, and was later led by anthropologist Miguel Vilar "and a team of renowned scientists . . . using cutting-edge genetic and computational technologies to analyze historical patterns in DNA from participants around the world to better understand our shared genetic roots." The ad claimed its DNA test could give customers a map of the migration trail that their distant ancestors took when they spread out from Africa, and Lily was excited to try it.

According to the Genographic Project, modern *Homo sapiens* lived in what is now eastern Africa over one hundred thousand years ago. By some estimates, groups of early humans left the continent between seventy and forty thousand years ago and began to populate the rest of the world. Many of them interbred

> **" "** Through decades of research and reporting, National Geographic seeks to answer and share fundamental questions about our collective past: how our ancestors migrated from our African homeland, adapted, and populated the Earth. With your help, we are writing this ever-evolving story."

—National Geographic Genographic Project

with other subspecies of archaic humans, such as Neanderthals, as they migrated. Some early humans traveled north and west to what is now Europe, and others settled in central Asia or migrated east, across deserts and mountains. Some ventured along coastlines and frozen landmasses and some may have even crossed oceans by boat until they reached the Pacific Islands and the Americas.

Lily requested a mitochondrial DNA (mtDNA) test in February 2007. Mitochondrial DNA, located outside the nucleus of the cell, passes unchanged from mother to child, and allows people to trace their matrilineal ancestral patterns. (In general, fathers pass no mitochondria to the offspring.) The Genographic Project also offers a Y-chromosome DNA test that traces the patrilineal patterns through random sequence variants on the Y chromosome. By analyzing mitochondria and Y-chromosome DNA sequences and identifying mutations, the project sorts participants into clusters based on similar patterns in their DNA sequence. Ann Turner, who independently analyzes customers' DNA sequences, explains, "The broad clusters are known as haplogroups, and the divisions between haplogroups occurred tens of thousands of years ago." These haplogroups represent the genetic identity of a person's parental ancestry.

In March 2007, Lily received her mitochondrial DNA kit and swabbed her cheek. She sealed the swab tip inside the return package and mailed it back the next day. When her results came in May, she discovered that her matrilineal line belonged to haplogroup K, which dates to about twenty-five thousand years ago, when this group split off from the larger haplogroup U. She traced her finger along the line her matrilineal ancestors traveled, going north from eastern Africa and across what is now Egypt, and then turning west through present-day Jordan, Syria, and into Turkey. From there, haplogroup K migrated into what is now western Europe.

Lily discovered that she could transfer her results online to FamilyTreeDNA and choose to be "matched" with other people in her haplogroup. As more people signed up for the mtDNA testing, Lily received email notices that she had haplogroup matches—954 of them, so far. That meant she shared a common ancestor with each one of these participants. Lily was frustrated to learn, however, that their most recent common ancestor lived so many generations back that she probably wouldn't appear in anyone's family tree. According to the FamilyTreeDNA forum, "A low resolution match means that you have about a 50 percent chance of sharing a common ancestor within the last 52 generations (about 1,300 years), and a high-resolution match reduces the figure to around 28 generations (about 700 years)."

Not many families have a record of ancestors that goes back to the fourteenth century or earlier. Some families, if they're lucky enough to find birth, death, marriage, or census records through online, library, or historical institute archives, can trace their ancestry back multiple generations. Other families cannot. You might have an ancestor who was adopted or born out of wedlock, for example, and family documents might be missing. Or your ancestors might have been enslaved, and their names, marriages,

Two hikers squat next to Ötzi, Europe's oldest natural mummy. Because Ötzi's body was so well preserved, researchers can study Ötzi's DNA and the frozen bacteria in his intestines.

and births went unrecorded. Finding documentation of ancestry can be challenging.

Lily could not find a common ancestor with any of her matches on FamilyTreeDNA in her own family's records, but she did join a project that told her more about Haplogroup K. She learned that people in this haplogroup are related to Ötzi, a.k.a. the Iceman, the frozen mummy of a man who lived somewhere between 3400 and 3100 BCE. In 1991 Ötzi was discovered in the Ötztal Alps, on the border between Austria and Italy, by two German hikers who thought the body was a hiker who had died. After authorities rescued the body from the ice, medical examiners and archaeologists determined it to be about five thousand years old. Ötzi's discovery was reported in newspapers all over the world. Lily had read about it at the time and was fascinated by the story. So she was excited to find out that Ötzi was one of her very distant relatives.

EXPANDED DIRECT-TO-CONSUMER TESTING

In 2007 the popular website 23andMe started offering direct-to-consumer genetic testing that would report both ancestry and health information from DNA within a saliva sample. Instead of swabbing their cheeks, customers collected saliva by spitting into a sample tube. For less than $100, 23andMe would provide users with risk assessments on 254 diseases and conditions, including breast cancer and Alzheimer's disease. Customers were excited to be able to take DNA tests and to know how their genetic variants might put them at risk for diseases.

Many doctors, however, question the accuracy of direct-to-consumer genetic testing. They also point out the limitations of this type of gene testing. For example, 23andMe analyzes only two mutations in the *BRCA1* gene and one variant in the *BRCA2*

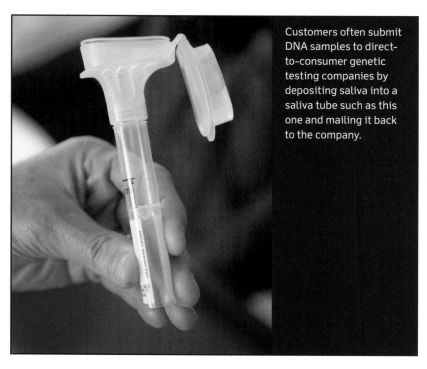

Customers often submit DNA samples to direct-to-consumer genetic testing companies by depositing saliva into a saliva tube such as this one and mailing it back to the company.

DNA OF MAN'S BEST FRIEND

In 2018 a reporter for NBC 5 Chicago investigated different direct-to-consumer genetic testing companies by sending in two different DNA samples. The first sample was his own saliva, and the testing companies reported quite different ancestry percentages. So the reporter sent in a second DNA sample, from an unusual customer—his Labrador retriever named Bailey. Most of the testing companies reported that Bailey's sample was unreadable, which was an expected result coming from a human DNA testing company. But one company, Orig3n, failed to report that the customer was not human. The company sent results saying that Bailey's "muscle force would probably be great for quick movements like boxing and basketball, and that she has the cardiac output for long endurance bike rides or runs," the reporter wrote.

gene, all associated with an increased risk of developing certain cancers. Doctors argue that this testing is incomplete because more than one thousand identified *BRCA* mutations have health implications. More complete testing is available, but it requires a doctor's prescription.

Doctors also questioned the ethics of online reporting of important medical information to customers who may not be educated in health care. They were concerned about what happens when a customer learns they have a pathogenic genetic variant associated with a serious illness. These websites typically don't offer avenues for customers to speak to doctors about the results of their tests. Or, if a direct-to-consumer test finds no pathogenic variants, the customer might not know that they could still carry an untested variant and be at risk for developing the medical condition or for passing along an unidentified variant to their child. Also, it isn't clear how up to date or complete the medical information on direct-to-consumer testing websites is. Customers might be misled or misinformed.

Although the testing websites include language to explain that their results are not meant to diagnose medical conditions, customers might still believe their results are proof they have or don't have an illness. Doctors who specialize in these medical conditions know that a person's risk for developing disease can be influenced as much by lifestyle and environment as by inherited factors. A result showing an increased risk for a particular disease does not mean you will develop it. Likewise, the absence of such a result does not mean you are free from all risk of developing the disease. The medical community is continually discovering new information about both pathogenic and benign gene variants. But new findings in genetic studies are reported in medical journals that may not be easily available or understandable to the general public. Direct-to-consumer testing companies often list their literature sources, but they do not always inform their customers of their updates. Customers may not learn about new findings unless they go to a doctor or carry out their own research through such medical literature databases as OMIM or PubMed.

GENETIC TESTING REVOLUTION

Since 2007 other companies have jumped into the business of direct-to-consumer DNA testing. These include Ancestry, MyHeritage, African Ancestry, Living DNA, Helix, Orig3n, and many more. From these popular tests, people may learn some information about their genetic ancestry and possibly their family history. Ancestral reporting, however, is limited by each company's database of collected DNA samples. The majority (about 80 percent) of participants on Ancestry and similar

> **❝** Our results demonstrate the importance of confirming [direct-to-consumer] raw data variants in a clinical laboratory that is well versed in both complex variant detection and classification."
>
> —Stephany Leigh Tandy-Connor et al, *Genetics in Medicine*, 2018

platforms have been of European ancestry. So the results for someone of Irish descent, for example, could be very specific to a region in Ireland, whereas results for someone from African or Asian descent may be vague or even misleading.

One company, African Ancestry, specifically serves the African American community and helps customers determine specific African countries and ethnic groups of origin dating back more than five hundred years. Both 23andMe and the Genographic Project have launched efforts to collect samples from people in underrepresented countries. And other companies have tried to improve their reports through increased sample diversity by marketing to minority communities in the Unites States. But some of their efforts, however, have led to controversy.

In 2019 Ancestry created a television ad showing a white man encouraging a black woman in the pre-Civil War South to flee north with him to freedom. The ad attempted to portray a couple in love, with the white man offering an engagement ring. Ancestry was forced to remove the ad from television and YouTube after historians, bioethicists, African American genetic genealogists, and the general public criticized it and pointed out its misrepresentation of the American history of slavery.

Arthur Caplan, professor of bioethics at the New York University Langone Medical Center, commented on the ad, "I think it's a historically horrific ad. It either reflects an utter ignorance or a willful ignorance of American history. They are trying to lure in customers with the idea that there were these hidden romances, making that claim in a sea of slavery and Jim Crow."

Ancestry apologized for the ad, stating, "Ancestry is committed to telling important stories from history. This ad was intended to represent one of those stories. We very much appreciate the feedback we have received and apologize for any offense that the ad may have caused."

The lack of diversity in DNA databases is found not only in ancestral DNA testing but also in medical genetic testing and research. Many people of color are reluctant to take genetic tests for ancestral or medical testing because of America's history with eugenics, the medical industry's negligence of minorities, and law enforcement's frequent misuse of DNA samples. Vox journalist Brian Resnick writes about the disparity this way, "It's adding to the long-standing problem of people of color being excluded from medical research. And it could also end up increasing health care disparities in America—which are already stark and stubborn."

RECEIVING UNEXPECTED OR UPSETTING RESULTS

In addition to learning about the limitations of ancestral reporting, some direct-to-consumer genetic test customers might receive information that is often difficult or painful to comprehend. Imagine taking a DNA test and discovering that your father is not your biological parent or that you have half siblings you never knew you had. That happened to Jason White, from Shreveport, Louisiana. In a January 2019 television interview with ABC's *Good Morning America*, Jason reported calling 23andMe to discuss his unsettling DNA test results. "The operator told me that I wouldn't be the first one to find out that I had a father or a different family than I thought. She said it's happened quite often," White said.

One woman, Catherine St. Clair of Texas, was so unsettled after learning that she and her father were not biologically related that she formed a closed Facebook group called DNA NPE Friends. NPE stands for "Not Parent Expected." Here, people can share their stories about learning the truth about their parents. The group has thousands of members and is still expanding.

Some people using DNA testing have learned that they were adopted or that they have multiple half siblings who share the same sperm donor. Twenty-year-old photographer Eli Baden-Lasar was conceived by anonymous sperm donation, and he discovered he had thirty-two half siblings from the same donor. He located his half siblings, spent time with them, and took their portraits, some of which were published in the *New York Times*. "It felt a bit embarrassing to be asking for their time," Baden-Lasar said. "One guy responded to a message and gave me an afternoon; he said, 'I'll do it for you because of blood,' as a joke."

Others have discovered they had children they don't know, as in the case of sperm donors who match with their biological children. Some people who have frozen their embryos for future implantation have discovered that their fertility clinic mistakenly implanted their embryos in another person's womb. This means they have biological children who were born to different parents. African Americans whose ancestry composition includes African and European regions have reported the emotional difficulty of receiving DNA proof that their ancestors were sexually violated and abused.

Customer representatives from Ancestry and 23andMe are trained extensively in DNA science and in talking to customers, but they are not psychotherapists. After speaking with representatives, customers might feel empowered to look further into their new family connections, or they may feel emotionally vulnerable.

WHAT IS A SINGLE NUCLEOTIDE POLYMORPHISM (SNP)?

A polymorphism is a common DNA sequence variation, and so a single nucleotide polymorphism is a variation of a single nucleotide in the sequence. We all have polymorphisms that are related to our traits, such as hair and eye color, and to our ancestry. These polymorphisms usually do not cause inherited disease. However, they can sometimes contribute to disease susceptibility and affect how we respond to medicines. The difference between a polymorphism and a mutation is in its frequency in the population. If the allele is found in 1 percent or more of the population, it is considered a polymorphism. If its frequency is less than 1 percent, the variant is considered a mutation. Direct-to-consumer genetic testing results usually report a customer's SNPs.

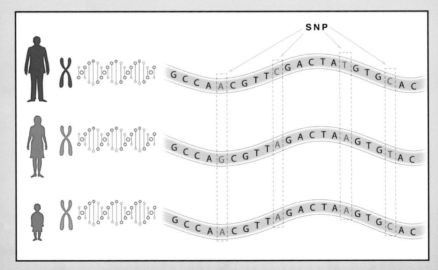

This diagram illustrates how SNPs might occur in a genetic sequence. For the same sequence in two individuals, single nucleotides might differ (such as the A indicated in the top strand and the G in the middle strand). Offspring might inherit either parent's SNPs.

The testing companies do caution customers that they may receive information they do not expect. Customers of 23andMe are asked to opt in before receiving their health results. The company has a page telling customers how to find a genetic counselor if they are concerned about their health. Ann Wojcicki, founder of 23andMe, argues for letting customers decide what to do with their test results. "Making this kind of test directly available to consumers is a huge milestone in empowering people to be in control of their own health information. . . . While doctors and genetic counselors play an important role in delivering health care and health information, I am an advocate for consumers having more direct access to personalized information so they can take charge of their health."

Some customers might agree with that statement. Others might agree *before* they receive unexpected news but then change their mind. Nancy Wurtzel thought she was prepared for her 23andMe test results until she learned she had a gene variant that put her at an increased risk for Alzheimer's disease. Both of her parents died of the disease. Receiving the results was a shock. "I wished someone was there to listen to what I was feeling at the time," she says. "I don't advise anyone to do it by themselves."

ANOTHER DOWNSIDE OF DIRECT-TO-CONSUMER DNA TESTING

Before customers buy genetic tests for ancestral or medical reporting, they may want to consider other possible outcomes. Sometimes third parties have access to the results of these private DNA tests. Many of these testing companies, including Ancestry and 23andMe, admit to selling DNA test results to pharmaceutical companies that are working on developing drugs for medical conditions. Customers receive information about this and must opt in before purchase, and their data is cleared of any identifying features so the pharmaceutical companies won't know whose DNA they're using. But current laws do not require those companies to share their profits with the people whose DNA they used.

Although it is illegal for health insurers in the United States to use the results of a direct-to-consumer genetic test (or any other genetic test) to deny coverage or require you to pay higher premiums, the Genetic Information Nondiscrimination Act does not apply to insurance policies offered by companies that have fewer than fifteen employees or to such other forms of insurance as disability insurance, long-term care insurance, or life insurance. Companies that offer these policies can ask employees for the results of any genetic testing they may have taken. Some job applicants fear that employers might consider them a risk to hire if their genetic testing shows they have a predisposition to a chronic or terminal illness. It is still unclear how employees may or may not be protected from discrimination based on genetic testing results.

Some of these genetic testing companies provide customers' DNA to law enforcement, and that is currently legal. Police departments around the country have uploaded DNA samples from crime scenes to FamilyTreeDNA and GEDmatch to pinpoint suspects by matching them to genetic cousins who contributed DNA samples on the websites. This technology has helped solve violent crimes, but it also has the potential to incriminate innocent people because of errors in DNA processing or interpretation.

66 Currently, there aren't any laws that regulate how law enforcement employs long-range familial searching, which hobbyists and do-gooders have turned to for years to find the biological families of adoptees. But some legal experts argue its use in criminal cases raises grave privacy concerns."

—Megan Molteni, *Wired*

LAW ENFORCEMENT AND ANCESTRY WEBSITES

In 2018 police began using novel methods to find violent criminals of unsolved crimes. They submitted raw DNA data files—reportedly DNA from old crime scenes—to GEDmatch, a free genealogy website that allows customers to upload DNA files to find family members. In one case, investigators created a fake profile for the notorious Golden State Killer, a serial killer suspected of multiple rapes and murders, and they uploaded a DNA file to GEDmatch. The DNA matched to a distant relative of the suspect, and the suspect was eventually arrested.

At the time, GEDmatch operators had no idea that their website was being used in this way. Their open-source platform is not legally protected. Some GEDmatch customers, upon hearing the story, were concerned about privacy and deleted their data from the platform. As of October 2019, according to NBC News, law enforcement used GEDmatch to solve more than fifty rapes and homicides in twenty-nine states. However, after customer concern persuaded GEDmatch to change their privacy rules and restrict law enforcement use of the database, such crimes have become harder to solve using DNA matching. "There are cases that won't get solved or will take longer to solve," said Lori Napolitano, the chief of forensic services at the Florida Department of Law Enforcement.

After the controversy went public, GEDmatch changed its policy and let customers choose whether to allow law enforcement access to their profile. Many chose not to give permission, citing privacy concerns. Law enforcement and genetic investigators complained, stating that their work is essential to keeping violent criminals from getting away with their crimes. At least one Florida state judge agreed with them, and in 2019 issued a warrant to force GEDmatch to allow police to search its database of over one million profiles. Customers wonder if judges could issue similar warrants to force 23andMe and Ancestry to allow police access to their even larger databases. 23andMe has said it will "use every legal remedy possible" to challenge such an order. The legal system might have to determine how and when a judge could issue a warrant, and if the searches are even legal in the first place.

Joseph James DeAngelo (*pictured here in an orange jumpsuit*) is suspected of being the notorious Golden State Killer who committed burglaries, rapes, and murders in California in the 1970s and 1980s. To collect DeAngelo's DNA discreetly, police extracted a used tissue that DeAngelo discarded in his curbside garbage bin and matched the DNA on the tissue to genetic samples from Golden State Killer crime scenes.

In December 2019, GEDmatch sold its company to Verogen, a leading manufacturer of lab equipment for DNA analysis that specializes in next-generation DNA testing services catered to law enforcement. Verogen has plans to update the quality of its website and services, and, at least for a time, will continue to allow customers to opt in or out of police searches.

In 2018, another story broke that police were using the FamilyTreeDNA website to catch criminals. Customers of this platform also became concerned about how to maintain their privacy. Some customers worry about being implicated in a crime they didn't commit. They have no control over the reliability of police forensics at a crime scene nor of a technician's analysis of a particular DNA sample. Crime scene samples can be contaminated, and technicians do make errors in interpreting a sample. Studies have shown a great variability in DNA sample analysis. "I don't think it's unreasonable to point out that DNA evidence is being used in a system that's had horrible problems with evidentiary reliability," says one public defender. Customers need to be aware of the risk to their privacy and to their freedom before they take a genetic test. As of 2019, FamilyTreeDNA continues to allow law enforcement to search its database but charges for this service and limits results.

COMPARING GENETIC TESTS

When Lily tried 23andMe in 2013, she wanted both ancestry and health-related results. After taking the new test and sending it back, she received an email from 23andMe saying that they could no longer provide medical results and would offer refunds. The email said, "At this time, we have suspended the health-related part of our service to comply with the [FDA]'s directive on November 22, 2013 to discontinue new consumer access during our regulatory review process. . . . We will not be able to provide you with access to the 23andMe health-related results from your purchase."

The FDA had concerns about the accuracy and the limitations of the medical information that 23andMe was giving customers and ordered the company to stop sending health interpretations of genetic information. Lily did not request a refund and instead waited for the ancestry information. She wanted to compare it to her information from other testing companies. She had also read online that customers could upload their raw DNA data from 23andMe to a site called Promethease, a literature-retrieval system that compares genetic data to an online encyclopedia of genetic research called SNPedia. Information on SNPedia is said to come from peer-reviewed, scientific publications. Lily wanted to see which of her gene variants would be highlighted on this platform so she could do her own health research. She had been diagnosed with an inherited immune deficiency, and she wanted to know if this illness ran in her family or was caused by a specific gene mutation that she carried.

Meanwhile, 23andMe negotiated with the FDA and asked for approval of its health data reporting. In October 2015, the company received FDA approval to report information on thirty-six rare diseases and conditions. By 2017, the FDA cleared 23andMe to report health risks associated with ten more conditions, including late-onset Alzheimer's disease, and in 2018 the company could begin reporting on three mutations of the *BRCA* gene that increase the risk of breast and prostate cancer. The company states on their reporting pages that the results do not include all possible genetic variants that affect these medical conditions and diseases. Lily could check her updated report for her own genetic health risks.

Lily researched different genetic testing companies and took more tests, including an Ancestry test and a free test from Genes for Good, a volunteer research program through the University of Michigan. She learned more about testing methodologies and understood that the genotyping methods used by 23andMe, Ancestry, and most other commercial direct-to-consumer DNA testing companies analyze only a small number of base pairs within specific tested genes. This technology is faster, cheaper, but much less extensive or medically informative than full sequencing on gene panels, or whole exome testing. Whole genome sequencing, which sequences your entire genome, had been so costly and time-consuming that it was unavailable until 2019 as a direct-to-consumer test.

Later, when Lily heard about a time-limited discount for a whole exome test through a company called Genos, she jumped at the chance. According to the Genos website, their method "sequence[s] over 20,000 genes which contain 85 [percent] of known disease-related variants. . . ." A Genos test could potentially provide a great deal more medically significant information than the 23andMe test, although Genos still only sequenced the exons of each gene. When Lily received her results from Genos, however, she soon discovered that its website was not a simple interface. She spent hours learning how the website worked and what the language meant. Then she looked closely at her genetic variants.

Lily's results showed that she had multiple benign variants and variants of uncertain significance. She also had pathogenic variants in thirty-eight different genes, associated with a disease or disorder. If she had not learned something about genetic testing by this point, she might have panicked about this result. She checked if the diseases were autosomal recessive, and then she looked at how many copies she had of each pathogenic variant to understand if they actually put her at risk for developing a medical condition. Lily had inherited only one copy of most of her pathogenic variants. That meant she was probably not at risk for the associated diseases.

Still, Lily researched each variant by linking from the Genos website to ClinVar, NIH's public archive of human variations and phenotypes. She read medical papers about her pathogenic variants but soon realized she didn't have the science background to understand the full implications of the papers she reviewed.

Lily had so many questions about her results that she decided to pay for a consultation with a genetic counselor. She used the contact form on the Genos website to make a phone appointment. Lily told the genetic counselor about her health complications, and the genetic counselor went through each of Lily's pathogenic variants with her over the phone. The good news was that the genetic counselor did not find variants that had an obvious impact on Lily's health. The counselor did tell Lily, however, that she was a carrier of gene variants associated with three rare inherited diseases. Those variants could affect Lily's children if they inherited her copy of the pathogenic variant and a second copy from their other parent.

After doing all of this genetic testing and research, Lily decided to compare her results from the different companies. That's when she noticed discrepancies in both her ancestral DNA results and her medical results. All the companies reported

SAMPLE GENOS RESULT

This is an example of the information Lily received from Genos about one of her thirty-eight pathogenic variants. This variant is associated with the autosomal recessive congenital disorder of glycosylation, type 1a.

> ### PMM2: c.470T>C (p.F157S)
>
> This type of variant is known as a SNP. Your DNA sequence is C where the reference genome sequence is T. You have 1 copy of this variant. It is located on the *PMM2* gene. This variant alters protein by changing the amino acid Phenylalanine (F) to a Serine (S).
>
> 0.050%-0.069%
>
> Population Frequency
>
> Found in 0% of people sequenced in the 1000 Genomes Project
>
> Found in 0% of people sequenced in the NHLBI Exome Sequencing Project
>
> This pathogenic variant of the *PMM2* gene was found in 0.050 to 0.069 percent of the people sequenced in the 1000 Genome Project, a "collaboration among research groups in the US, UK, China, and Germany to produce an extensive catalog of human genetic variation that will support future medical research studies." It showed up in Lily's results on Genos but not on 23andMe, which also tests the *PMM2* gene.

Lily to have European ancestry, but some companies pinpointed ancestral regions with more specificity. And the results varied so much that Lily was unsure what to believe.

More interesting, or concerning, were the discrepancies in Lily's health results. Lily had a medically significant gene variant in her 23andMe results that did not show up in her Genos report.

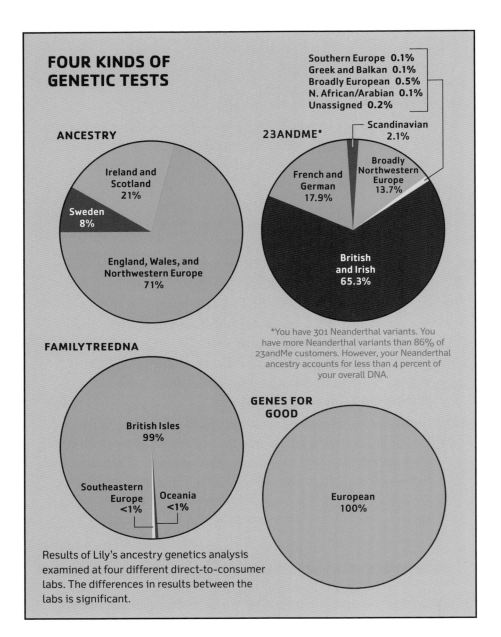

FOUR KINDS OF GENETIC TESTS

Southern Europe 0.1%
Greek and Balkan 0.1%
Broadly European 0.5%
N. African/Arabian 0.1%
Unassigned 0.2%

ANCESTRY

Ireland and Scotland 21%

Sweden 8%

England, Wales, and Northwestern Europe 71%

23ANDME*

Scandinavian 2.1%

Broadly Northwestern Europe 13.7%

French and German 17.9%

British and Irish 65.3%

*You have 301 Neanderthal variants. You have more Neanderthal variants than 86% of 23andMe customers. However, your Neanderthal ancestry accounts for less than 4 percent of your overall DNA.

FAMILYTREEDNA

British Isles 99%

Southeastern Europe <1%

Oceania <1%

GENES FOR GOOD

European 100%

Results of Lily's ancestry genetics analysis examined at four different direct-to-consumer labs. The differences in results between the labs is significant.

When Lily called Genos to ask if she carried the pathogenic variant (associated with a disorder called hemochromatosis) that showed up on her 23andMe results, the Genos representative was surprised about the discrepancy. Genos checked Lily's data and called her back to say that she did indeed carry that gene variant. The representative could not explain why this variant did not show up in her results. Genos promised that all customers would soon see refreshed results after their technology update. But that pathogenic variant for hemochromatosis was still missing from Lily's updated report. Lily also contacted 23andMe to check if her result for this variant was accurate. And 23andMe reanalyzed Lily's DNA results and reported that her medical information had not changed.

These discrepancies made Lily question the reliability of her results. Much of the variation in interpretation is because of the lack of full understanding of each gene and each variant's effect on that gene's expression. Both companies tell their customers not to use their reports to diagnose a medical condition, but they don't say that their tests could be inaccurate or that reporting could be inconsistent across platforms.

Scientists have recently studied the results of direct-to-consumer testing and found them to be unreliable. The March 2018 issue of *Genetics in Medicine* published results from a small study that concluded that 40 percent of the variants reported by direct-to-consumer genetic tests turned out to be false positives: abnormalities reported that were not actually there. The study also noted that eight variants reported as pathogenic on direct-to-consumer test results are benign. Stephany Leigh Tandy-Connor, study leader at Ambry Genetics Corp in the US, said, "Such a high rate of false positives in this particular study was unexpected. . . . While [direct-to-consumer] results may lead to healthy changes in lifestyle or diet, these could also result in unwarranted emotions, including anxiety when someone obtains unexpected information, inaccurate information, or disappointment when receiving a lack of comprehensive diagnostic analysis."

After all her direct-to-consumer genetic testing, Lily was

careful about trusting her results. She read that companies were offering DNA tests that purport to tell you the best diet, nutritional supplements, and exercise for your genotype. But then she read that so far scientific reports indicate that eating for your genotype shows no health benefit. Lily thought these tests might

DNA TESTING FOR ADOPTEES

Katherine was adopted in Colombia, South America, where she was born and where her American parents once worked. She grew up in the United States, knew she was adopted from an early age, and went back to Colombia when she was an adult. There, people kept telling her she looked as if she was from this or that region of the country. That made her curious about her ancestry, so she took a 23andMe DNA test. She wasn't thinking much about connecting with relatives at first. She was more interested in her ancestry composition, which showed her to be about 50 percent from an indigenous population, and the rest from the Iberian Peninsula (an area including Spain and Portugal) with a small percentage of Ashkenazi Jewish ancestry.

Later, one of her matched distant cousins reached out to her on 23andMe and told her he was adopted too. Months after that, Katherine discovered another cousin who shared even more DNA segments. They connected online, and then met in person and talked for hours. "It's exciting. It's weird," Katherine said of meeting her biological relatives. "You meet these random people and you connect!" Katherine's cousin introduced her to other family members, and they talked about life in Colombia, and how they all came to the United States. "They were so welcoming. . . . They were the nicest people," Katherine said. She knows that not all family meetings go as well for adoptees. Some learn sad stories about their families. But Katherine's experience has been positive. "To find these cousins was life-changing," she said. "And it wouldn't have happened had I not done that test."

be trendy and fun but were also a marketing ploy to make money for the testing companies.

Still, to learn about her own risk for certain cancers, including breast and ovarian cancer, and heart disease, Lily ordered a genetic test from Color, a reputable medical testing company that works with the All of Us Research Program at NIH. Color uses gene panels that fully sequence selected genes associated with the targeted illnesses. Her results from thirty sequenced genes did not indicate an increased genetic risk of hereditary cancer. However, because of a family history of melanoma, Lily was advised to have more frequent medical exams and mammograms. The results of her heredity heart health test also showed no increased genetic risk for heart disease. Color did suggest, however, that people who have a family history of heart disease, as Lily does, might consider evaluation by a cardiologist. Through Color, Lily had the option of scheduling either a genetics counselor appointment to discuss any genetic risks or a pharmacist appointment to discuss how she would metabolize certain medicines, based on her genetics. But she didn't think she needed to do this.

After testing with Color, Lily decided to take one more DNA test for possible medical information. When Veritas Genetics launched its direct-to-consumer whole genome testing service in 2019 and offered a deep discount for the first one thousand customers, Lily ordered one. Her order had to be approved by a doctor, and Lily chose to work with a physician through Veritas Genetics. Lily waited about four months for her results from the time of her order. Her results told her she was a carrier of variants associated with three autosomal recessive disorders, which she already knew from her whole exome test. She found no genetic mutation for her inherited immune deficiency, but she learned how she would metabolize certain medicines. She could use this information if her doctors ever prescribed one of them. Veritas Genetics also reported on Lily's specific physical traits influenced by her genotype such as muscle strength, reaction to caffeine, sensory perception, metabolism, and more. These were interesting facts, but Lily was not sure to what extent they impacted her health. When she went back to the Veritas website to reread her report in December 2019, she learned that the company was suspending business in the US for lack of funding.

As Lily thought about her genetic testing results, she came away with a confirmation of something else she already knew— that health was based on both genetics and lifestyle. Lily may have an increased risk for certain conditions she didn't yet have, but she may also be able to offset those risks with a healthy diet, an exercise program, good sleep habits, and stress reduction. And if, going forward, her health worsened, she'd call a doctor and, perhaps, share her genetic results.

CHAPTER 7
GENETIC REVOLUTION— TWENTY-FIRST CENTURY AND BEYOND

Genetic testing and analysis have brought about a revolution in health care. In 2003, when the Human Genome Project announced its completion, whole genome sequencing was not part of most medical diagnoses or treatment plans. As genome testing became more efficient and less expensive, doctors gained a new diagnostic tool. By 2019, only sixteen years later, the cost to generate a whole genome sequence for an individual dropped from $150 million to less than $1,000. Inexpensive DNA sequencing has already generated a massive amount of genetic information and has led to advancements in the field of gene therapy.

Gene therapy, treatment to modify pathogenic DNA sequences, has been tried in the United States for several decades with limited success. In 1990 at NIH, a four-year-old girl, Ashanti DeSilva, was successfully treated with gene therapy for a form of severe combined immunodeficiency (SCID), a genetic disorder that made her body unable to fight infections. Twenty-seven years later, the FDA approved the first gene therapy for treatment of a form of leukemia. By the end of 2017, two more gene therapy treatments were approved, and genetic scientists were eager to find more cures for patients with inherited disorders.

Genetic scientists are working on different gene therapy methods for treating sickle cell disease, an inherited disorder that affects red blood cells. Sickle cell disease is the most common inherited blood disorder in the United States, and it affects about one in five hundred African Americans and one in one thousand to fourteen hundred Hispanic Americans. It is also common in Americans of Middle Eastern, South Asian, and Mediterranean descent. These gene therapy methods involve genetically altering the patient's hematopoietic stem cells. These cells are from the bone marrow and can become new red blood cells.

CORRECTING AN ERROR IN THE GENETIC CODE

Jennelle Stephenson was born with sickle cell disease. She has been in and out of hospitals all her twenty-eight-year life and thought she would die early because she saw younger friends with the disease pass away. Sickle cell disease affects people like Stephenson who were born with two mutated copies of the beta globin gene (*HBB*). Beta globin is an essential component of hemoglobin that binds oxygen in red blood cells.

In people with sickle cell disease, some of their red blood cells, which carry oxygen throughout the body, are rigid and sickle-shaped instead of being round and flexible. These misshapen blood cells are less effective at delivering oxygen to tissues and can cluster and become stuck in small blood

CREATING SEX CELLS FROM OTHER HUMAN CELLS

At the beginning of the twenty-first century, scientists began experimenting with ways to create an embryo from such human cells as skin and blood cells. In 2006 Japanese Nobel laureate Shinya Yamanaka found a way to turn any human cell into induced pluripotent stem cells (iPS cells). These can be reprogrammed to become any kind of cell in the body. In 2016, researchers at Kyoto University in Japan announced they had turned cells from a mouse's tail into iPS cells, and then they made those into sex cells, which gestated as mouse pups. A group of international scientists is trying to replicate this process for human cells. They want to reprogram human iPS cells into sperm and egg cells. A team of researchers from Spain reported in 2016 that they were able to turn human iPS cells into sperm cells. This work was carried out at Stanford University in California, and the results were published in the online journal *Nature*.

But the complex process has not yet been repeated. As of 2019 human skin cells have been transformed into germ cells, which could develop into a sperm or egg. But so far, these do not have the ability to fertilize. If scientists are successful in turning human iPS cells into viable sperm and egg cells, couples who otherwise cannot have children, including many gay couples and infertile couples, could possibly conceive a child without a sperm or egg donor. And people may one day be able to have a child on their own without a partner or sperm donor. But all of this is still at least a decade away, according to Amander Clark, a stem cell biologist at UCLA, who is working in this area of research. "I do think we're less than 10 years away from making research-grade gametes," she says.

Even then, more research would be needed to understand the possible health implications for babies conceived by these methods. And there may be legal restraints on this work in countries where the creation of artificial embryos is not allowed.

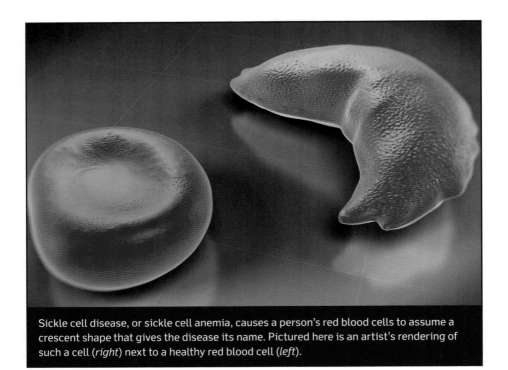

Sickle cell disease, or sickle cell anemia, causes a person's red blood cells to assume a crescent shape that gives the disease its name. Pictured here is an artist's rendering of such a cell (*right*) next to a healthy red blood cell (*left*).

vessels, further robbing organs of oxygen. The disease can cause infections, anemia, strokes, organ failure, and episodes of severe pain. Doctors have some medical options to help their patients with sickle cell disease, such as pain medications, blood transfusions, and bone marrow transplants, but in most patients, the disease continues to be debilitating.

On CBS's *60 Minutes* in March 2019, Stephenson told physician and chief medical correspondent Jonathan LaPook about how her condition affected her with agonizing pain. "It's a very sharp, like, stabbing, [it] almost feels like bone-crushing pain," she said. She remembered one time when she went to the hospital and collapsed on the floor in agony, but doctors did not help her. They thought she was faking pain to get narcotics.

After suffering for over two decades, Stephenson was one of a few patients to join an NIH clinical trial for a novel gene replacement therapy for sickle cell disease patients. To treat this disease, NIH hematologist John F. Tisdale and his colleagues developed a therapy involving viruses, which act as a vector, or carrier, to transfer healthy DNA into a patient's cells. First, doctors take an HIV virus and alter it so it can't cause disease. Then they insert a functioning *HBB* gene into the virus. The patient's bone marrow stem cells are removed, and in the laboratory, they are combined with the virus that carries the functioning DNA. Later, the patient is infused with the patient's own stem cells that have been treated. If the therapy is successful, these stem cells start producing healthy red blood cells in the patient. The treatment is both complicated and risky.

In 2017 Stephenson spent a month in the hospital to have this therapy and then went home to Florida to recover. She returned to NIH for follow-up visits. Nine months after treatment, her new red blood cells were normal, and she reported feeling strong. Before her treatment she had to be careful not to exhaust herself, but these days she can go running, practice jujitsu, and live a healthy life.

Stephenson wasn't the only sickle cell patient at NIH to get well on this new gene therapy. Eight other patients also had this treatment and are responding well. According to a March 12, 2019, NIH press release, "Preliminary findings suggest that the approach has an acceptable level of safety and might help patients consistently produce normal red blood cells instead of the sickle-shaped ones that mark this painful, life-threatening disease."

NOT A SIMPLE TREATMENT

Before scientists can devise an appropriate gene therapy, they must understand the biological mechanism of the disease they hope to cure. Each disorder has many variables that play a role in the disease. Researchers must determine, for example, whether the best gene-therapy approach would be to edit the pathogenic sequence of the disease-causing gene, or increase the expression of (upregulate) another gene, which could lessen the negative health effects of the disease gene. They must also assess whether to correct the disease DNA in every cell, as in gene-therapy cancer treatments, or if correcting the DNA in a percentage of the patient's cells is sufficient for an effective treatment.

Genetic researchers also must consider the best way to deliver healthy DNA into the cells of the patient. A common approach has been to use deactivated viruses that would spread the healthy DNA in patient cells but not cause disease, as in Stephenson's treatment. But choosing the right virus can be difficult. Some viral vectors work well to enter the cell but are not effective at integrating permanently in the host DNA. Other viral vectors integrate well but may also affect other genes. Doctors must fully understand the function of the gene they want to correct, the interplay of that gene with other genes, and the biological mechanism of the viral vector they want to use in the therapy.

This is why gene therapy trials take years, even decades, before they result in an effective treatment—if they ever do. These trials are also controlled by regulatory agencies that establish safety guidelines and make sure that therapy does not affect the gametes of the patient. This safety measure is to make sure genetic changes are not passed down to future generations.

Despite recent successes, gene therapy is not without risk. In the past, patients have died from an immune response to the virus vectors or have developed cancer from the effects of gene therapy. Scientists have since made many improvements to lower the risk of dangerous side effects, but more work must be done before gene therapy can be declared completely safe. Before Stephenson received her new stem cells, she had to have chemotherapy to

COMPUTER SCIENCE AND GENOMIC SEQUENCING

Genetic research and advances over the past two decades have changed biological science and medicine. None of it would have been possible without the parallel development of digital technology and computer science. In the past, genetic scientists and clinical geneticists consulted such books as the *Mendelian Inheritance in Man*. Currently, they can check the public website OMIM, which catalogs all human genes and diseases and is regularly updated. Instead of consulting books with images of patients with inherited syndromes, doctors can use software programs that analyze facial features and offer suggested diagnoses (face2gene.com). And NGS would be impossible without computers to analyze the massive data generated by a single sample of DNA. Current computer software and sequencing programs can align DNA, RNA, and protein sequences and make analysis simple and informative. Computer science and genomic sequencing are forever linked.

clear out old cells in her bone marrow. This affected her immune system, and she had to be careful about not getting an infection while she stayed in the hospital. It also affected her reproductive system, and she will no longer be able to become pregnant. She understood the enormous medical risks and side effects and measured them against her high risk for dying young. "I never felt like a test subject," she said. "I just felt like a human being looking for a cure for sickle cell, and they did an amazing job."

The gene therapy treatment for sickle cell disease is still under review. Tisdale and his colleagues may need many more years of research and development to improve the treatment to make it more widely available. Future treatment for sickle cell disease may work without the need for chemotherapy.

Francis Collins, director of the NIH, is hopeful that scientists will develop gene therapy for other disorders that have few good treatments. "There are 7,000 genetic diseases for which we know the precise DNA misspelling," he says. "Couldn't this same strategy, this same set of principles, work for lots of those, maybe someday [even] all of them?"

Researchers and patients alike have questions about the risks of gene therapy and about the long-term effects of changing the human genome. But if gene therapy can cure more patients like Stephenson, doctors and patients both may continue to put their hope in this twenty-first-century cure.

GENE EDITING TOOLS

To address some of the challenges of gene therapy, a team of geneticists created a tool called CRISPR-Cas9 that can edit the human genome directly. CRISPR stands for clustered regularly interspaced short palindromic repeats. These repeats are found

LIGHT-ACTIVATED VECTORS

In 2019 scientists from Nanjing and Xiamen Universities in China experimented with using two types of light to deliver CRISPR-Cas9 gene-editing tools into mice, as an alternative to the virus vector. The goal of their experiment was to reduce the size of a tumor inside of a mouse. The researchers injected a CRISPR-Cas9 tool directly into a cancer tumor in the mouse. Then they shone near-infared radiation onto the skin covering the location where the tumor and the gene-editing tool were. When the radiation was absorbed, it converted to ultraviolet light. The ultraviolet light then cut molecules in the carrier package, releasing the CRISPR-Cas9 tool to activate tumor suppression and shrink the tumor. The researchers believe that their experiment proved to be both effective and safe.

CRISPR TECHNOLOGY

1

defective DNA strand

Scientists identify a defective DNA strand to be cut out and modified.

2

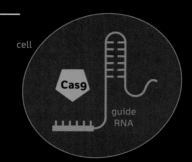

cell

Cas9

guide
RNA

They create guide RNA that has the same genomic code as the defective DNA. This is combined in a cell with an enzyme called Cas9, which acts like scissors to cut the defective DNA.

3

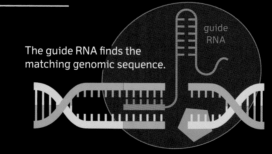

The guide RNA finds the matching genomic sequence.

guide
RNA

Then the Cas9 cuts the strand making a break in the DNA helix.

4

healthy DNA strand

Cells are able to detect and repair broken DNA. A healthy strand of DNA is inserted at the cut site, and enzymes repair it.

naturally in bacteria and are part of the system that bacteria use to fight viral infections. CRISPR are copies of small pieces of DNA from viruses that have once infected the bacteria. Viral DNA sequences are copied into short pieces of RNA. The RNA then binds with Cas9, a natural enzyme, and together they search for any new invading virus with similar DNA to the CRISPR. When they locate it, the Cas9 protein cuts and destroys the viral DNA.

Scientists discovered they could use CRISPR-Cas9 in the laboratory to locate and edit DNA. They use guide RNA to match the specific DNA sequence—a mutation, for example—they want to edit. They attach this guide RNA to Cas9 to locate and snip the designated DNA. With this method, scientists can delete or insert pieces of DNA into cells with precision. According to biochemist Jennifer Doudna at the University of California, Berkeley, one of the inventors of this genome-editing tool, "The CRISPR technology allows scientists to make changes to the DNA in cells that could allow us to cure genetic disease."

CRISPR-Cas9 is currently being studied for the treatment of such inherited diseases as cystic fibrosis, hemophilia, and sickle cell disease. It is not, however, a simple laboratory technique. CRISPR-Cas9 can have unintended or off-target effects that researchers must understand before they can bring the technology to health care. Also, some genes that can cause one clinical disorder also play a role in other illnesses. Doctors don't want to edit pieces of DNA to help cure a specific disease only to discover that they have caused another type of health problem. That is one reason why researchers have been careful to work only on the somatic (nonsex) cells in humans. If they were to edit the DNA in human sex cells (germline cells), or in human embryos that were later implanted in a person's womb, the genetic changes could be passed down to a patient's children, possibly affecting their health.

PRIME EDITING

In October 2019, scientists at the Broad Institute in Cambridge, Massachusetts, announced their laboratory success with a refined gene-editing method called prime editing that makes rewriting genes easier and safer than with the CRISPR technique. With CRISPR, scientists must cut both strands of the double helix of DNA, and the technique can also introduce errors into the DNA sequence. "It's proven difficult to use these molecular scissors [CRISPR] to make precise DNA changes in most cell types," says David Liu, a biologist working at the Broad Institute.

With prime editing, scientists don't need to cut both strands but, instead, snip one strand of DNA at a precise point in the genome. Another advantage of prime editing is that scientists can use it on cells that don't often divide, such as nerve and brain cells. Parkinson's and Huntington's are two diseases caused by nervous system genes, and genetic surgeons could one day use prime editing to cure them.

Prime editing has not yet been used on people, and it will take time before scientists understand how well it works. But Liu and his team at the Broad Institute have already made more than 175 gene edits in mouse and human cells in the laboratory. And they have been able to repair the genetic mutations that cause sickle cell disease and Tay-Sachs disease. If prime editing works well, scientists could potentially use it with patients suffering from any of a number of genetic diseases.

But, as with CRISPR, the new method also comes with risk of misuse. "Gene editing, like many technologies, can, in principle, be put to nefarious use. Prime editing in that regard does not pose an added grave danger to the planet," says Fyodor Urnov at the University of California, Berkeley. "That said, now is not the time for a sense of false security, but rather added vigilance."

GENE EDITING MAKES AN UNETHICAL DEBUT

In November 2018, Chinese genetic researcher He Jiankui stunned the world by announcing at an international summit on genome editing that he had used CRISPR-Cas9 to genetically alter embryos with the intention of making babies resistant to HIV, the virus that can cause AIDS. He used this technology for eight couples who wanted babies that wouldn't contract HIV. In each case, the father was HIV-positive and the mother was HIV-negative. He Jiankui implanted genetically altered embryos into the wombs of eight mothers by in vitro fertilization (IVF). Out of the eight, only two mothers became pregnant. One of those two, Grace, gave birth to twin girls, Lulu and Nana.

He Jiankui explained that he had used CRISPR-Cas9 to alter a gene called *CCR5* that allows HIV to infect human cells. In a YouTube video, He Jiankui explained his work in more depth: "When Lulu and Nana were just a single cell, this surgery removed the doorway through which HIV enters to infect people. A few days later, before returning Lulu and Nana to Grace's womb, we checked how the gene surgery went, by whole genome sequencing. The results indicated that the surgery worked safely, as intended. . . . No gene was changed except the one to prevent HIV infection."

Despite He Jiankui's confidence in his work, he was severely criticized by others in the field for using an untested therapeutic method and for modifying germline cells. In scientific communities throughout the world, germline editing is considered unethical, and it is illegal in many countries, including the United States. Nobody yet knows of the unintended consequences of altering or deleting genes in germline cells that can be passed down to offspring. Because both Nana and Lulu have two altered copies of *CCR5*, their offspring would be carriers of this novel sequence.

Critics have argued that the Cas9 enzyme can stay active long after making its first cut and could cause unintended DNA deletions in the developing embryo. Others say that there was no medical necessity for this germline editing, and it may have made the babies more susceptible to West Nile virus, another illness associated with the same gene. They point out that effective medical therapies already exist for preventing transmission of HIV from parent to child and for protecting a person from the HIV virus, without the need for this type of gene editing.

He Jiankui may also have unintentionally altered the brain function of the babies. Alcino J. Silva, a neurobiologist at the University of California, Los Angeles (UCLA), who studies the role of the *CCR5* gene in the brain, says, "The simplest interpretation is that those mutations will probably have an impact on cognitive function in the twins."

He Jiankui, however, stands by his work and believes he helped these families prevent HIV infection of their babies and avoid imposing the negative stigma of HIV on their children. He Jiankui says, "For this specific case, I feel proud, actually."

In March 2019, a prominent group of eighteen genetic scientists spoke out against He Jiankui's experiment. This human experiment highlights the need for worldwide scientific agreement on the use of genomic medicine. Francis Collins of the NIH called for an international consensus on setting limits

66 It's gobsmackingly horrifying. The choice to do this, the informed consent, the actual experimental design, the burden of proof, the justification for targeting this particular gene—it's all subpar, it's all shockingly unprofessional and unethical. There are many, many layers of wrongness here."

—Jennifer Phillips, research biologist at
the University of Oregon Institute of Neuroscience

> **❝** We call for a global moratorium on all clinical uses of human germline editing—that is, changing heritable DNA (in sperm, eggs, or embryos) to make genetically modified children.
>
> "By 'global moratorium', we do not mean a permanent ban. Rather, we call for the establishment of an international framework in which nations, while retaining the right to make their own decisions, voluntarily commit to not approve any use of clinical germline editing unless certain conditions are met."
>
> —Eric Lander et al, "Adopt a Moratorium on Heritable Genome Editing"

for such research. "Without such limits," said Collins, "the world will face the serious risk of a deluge of similarly ill-considered and unethical projects. Should such epic scientific misadventures proceed, a technology with enormous promise for prevention and treatment of disease will be overshadowed by justifiable public outrage, fear, and disgust."

After He Jiankui made his surprise announcement, he was put on leave by his university. In December 2019, he pleaded guilty and was convicted by a Chinese court "for illegally carrying out human embryo gene-editing intended for reproduction, in which three genetically edited babies were born." He and two collaborators were fined and sentenced to prison.

In the same month, Collins called for a moratorium on germline editing. "A moratorium of at least five years on heritable human gene editing would provide us time to engage in proactive, rather than reactive, discussions about the future of such technology. . . . We must never allow our technology to eclipse our humanity."

GENETIC CORRECTION VS. GENETIC ENHANCEMENT

Long before and certainly since this CRISPR-Cas9 shake-up, scientists have called for review and discussion of the important differences between genetic correction, editing a rare mutation that could cause a severe, single-gene disease, and genetic enhancement, editing normal genes with the intent to introduce specific traits that "improve" a body or enhance capabilities.

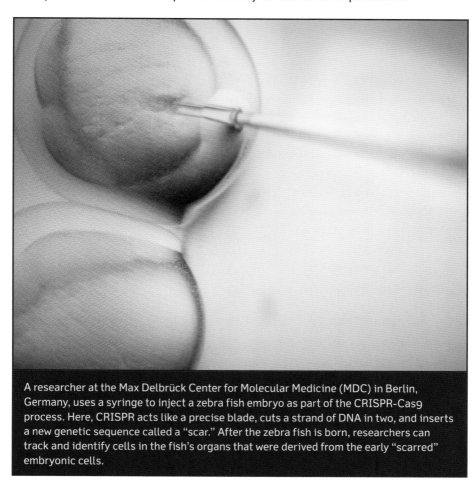

A researcher at the Max Delbrück Center for Molecular Medicine (MDC) in Berlin, Germany, uses a syringe to inject a zebra fish embryo as part of the CRISPR-Cas9 process. Here, CRISPR acts like a precise blade, cuts a strand of DNA in two, and inserts a new genetic sequence called a "scar." After the zebra fish is born, researchers can track and identify cells in the fish's organs that were derived from the early "scarred" embryonic cells.

DISCRIMINATION BASED ON PHYSIOLOGY

In 2019 South African Olympic gold medalist Caster Semenya lost her legal battle against World Athletics, which governs the sport of track. Semenya was contesting World Athletics eligibility regulations for athletes with differences in sexual development (DSD). This loss means that Semenya would have to start suppressing her naturally high testosterone levels if she wanted to compete in certain women's track events, including the 800-meter event in which she won gold at the 2012 and 2016 Summer Olympics. Taking medicine to lower her testosterone levels could affect not only Semenya's speed but also cause harmful medical side effects, and Semenya says she won't take it.

Caster Semenya wins gold in the Women's 800-meter final at the Gold Coast 2018 Commonwealth Games in Gold Coast, Australia.

In 2018 World Athletics had decided that an intersex condition called 46 XY DSD, which can result in elevated testosterone levels, gives female athletes who have this condition an unfair advantage. And World Athletics applied this rule to Semenya's case. So Semenya was subjected to genetic testing to determine her eligibility. The Court of Arbitration acknowledged that the new World Athletics rule is a form of discrimination but stated that "such discrimination is a necessary, reasonable, and proportionate means of achieving World Athletics's aim of preserving the integrity of female athletics in the restricted events."

Semenya and her lawyers argued that she should not have to alter her body with medication to compete. Other critics have pointed out that many athletes are lauded for their natural physiological advantages, but Semenya is barred from competing because of hers. "I just want to run naturally, the way I was born," Semenya said. "It is not fair that I am told I must change. It is not fair that people question who I am. I am Mokgadi Caster Semenya. I am a woman and I am fast."

Semenya's story is one of many that highlight discrimination based on physiology in the twenty-first century. Another example can be found in current US government policy debates. In 2018, for example, President Trump's administration was reported to be considering a law that would narrowly define gender as a biological, unchangeable condition determined by genitalia at birth. Such a law would define gender as either male or female, and any dispute about one's sex would have to be determined by genetic testing. If the US government passes such a law, it could remove legal protections for and violate the civil rights of more than 1.4 million transgender Americans, people who are a gender other than the one they were assigned at birth. The government has already tried to prevent transgender people from serving in the US military, and has legally challenged laws that could affect health care for this population, despite doctors saying that gender cannot be defined strictly by the appearance of a person's genitalia at birth.

"The idea that a person's sex is determined by their anatomy at birth is not true, and we've known that it's not true for decades," said Joshua D. Safer, an endocrinologist and executive director of the Center for Transgender Medicine and Surgery at Mount Sinai Health System in New York. Rather, research shows that gender identity is affected by multiple factors such as genetics, culture, and personal history.

Transgender people face discrimination, social stigma, and governmental restrictions in many countries with echoes of nineteenth- and twentieth-century eugenics. In many European countries, people who want to undergo hormone and surgical treatments related to being transgender have to accept a diagnosis of a mental disorder, or even be subjected to forced sterilization. In mid-April 2018, Portugal became only the sixth country in Europe, after Denmark, Ireland, Malta, Norway, and Belgium, to allow a legal change of gender without medical or state intervention. Government policy in Argentina allows transgender people to legally change their sex without medical intervention, but the same is not true for transgender people in Japan. In 2019, there was a global call for Japan to end its legal recognition policy for transgender people, which includes forced sterilization. In many countries, change has been slow. But in May 2019, the United Nations World Health Organization decided to change its manual of diagnoses and rename "gender identity disorders" to "gender incongruence," and it no longer lists this with mental disorders. This change may soon help transgender people who seek medical care to do so without doctors forcibly labeling them as mentally ill on the basis of their being transgender.

Semenya has said she won't defend her title in the 800-meter race in 2019 world championships. She is also appealing the ruling against her. Meanwhile, World Athletics will maintain its position that "there are some contexts, sport being one of them, where biology has to trump gender identity." Throughout the world, governing bodies of all kinds, not just in sports, legalize discrimination on the basis of physiology. Future scientific research may offer us the opportunity to understand our biologies in ways that will allow us to find our place—in athletics and in society more broadly.

66 I personally don't know that much about genetic testing and its uses medically, but I do take issue when something like it is actively used against people, like it was in [Semenya's] case. Certainly, the arena of sports still feels very separated when it comes to gender, whatever way you twist it, and I think some of the next steps that need to be taken are towards more acceptance and diversity in sports, be it through all-gender competitions or the recognition that gender isn't really binary, even on a biological level.

"Generally speaking, though, I understand, at a basic level, that genetic testing has an important place in biological science and, based on what I've heard from my doctors, there are studies looking into links between genetics and LGBTQ+ identities and in other relevant areas. And I support those studies to further our scientific understanding of the practice. I recently gave blood to a study about genetics at Boston Children's Hospital, after years of HRT (hormone replacement therapy) and the effects of that, but that's the only context in which I've ever specifically gotten a genetic test done. It was never required."

—Wendy, transgender student, aged seventeen

Doctors who are working on gene therapy carry out research for patients with diseases for which no good treatment options exist. They hope to improve the lives of their critically ill patients, or even to cure their diseases. Their health-care approach fits into the category of genetic correction. This type of human research is regulated in the United States, and treatments must be approved by the FDA before they are widely used. Society and the scientific community accept and approve of gene therapy research for critically ill patients.

In contrast, genetic enhancement of healthy people raises different societal and ethical concerns. Choosing personal traits—height, eye color, intellect, or athleticism, for example—by means of genetic testing and selection is controversial. Because the causes of human traits include not only genetics but also diet, lifestyle, and environmental exposure, such enhancements are inherently limited in their scope, and the ability to freely select one's traits is currently impossible. When American doctors take the Hippocratic oath, they make a promise before practicing medicine that says, "Above all, I must not play at God." Genetic scientists and doctors in other countries also abide by this principle. It is a moral question whether partaking in genetic enhancement violates this oath.

The next few decades will reveal how the world will use the science of gene therapy and genome editing. Will it be used only to cure disease, or will rogue scientists and doctors use genome editing and enhancement to change the human population? Who will have access to genetic correction and enhancement? And who determines which genetic corrections are medically necessary and which serve another goal? These pressing questions will need answers as we proceed into a new era of genetic medicine.

Imagine going into a doctor's office with your genetic test results so you and your doctor could tailor your treatment to your specific genetic and biological needs. You could discuss how your genes might affect your response to certain medicines, or if you need to change your diet or take certain vitamins because of a deficiency caused by your genes. When you are ready to have children, you could talk to your doctor about genetic testing for your baby. Or you might even take part in choosing which sperm and eggs to use for in vitro fertilization based on a careful selection of DNA, or even of desirable family traits. And when you grow old, you might be able to have genetic treatment to slow down your body's aging.

Some of these advancements are already here. Precision medicine is a novel approach to health care that accounts for an individual's genetics, lifestyle, diet, and environment. It has only become possible in the era of genomic testing, and it is still in its infancy. But as the field develops, many more patients may begin asking about individualized medicine for their genome.

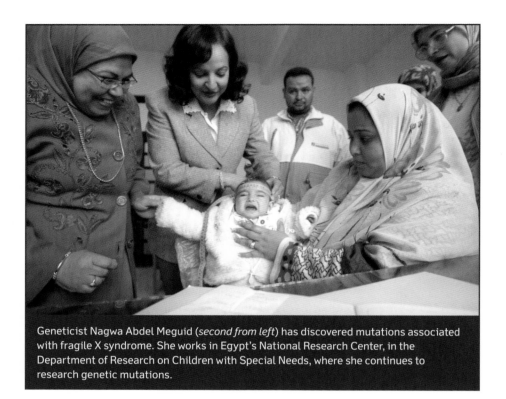

Geneticist Nagwa Abdel Meguid (*second from left*) has discovered mutations associated with fragile X syndrome. She works in Egypt's National Research Center, in the Department of Research on Children with Special Needs, where she continues to research genetic mutations.

For instance, doctors can tailor specific cancer treatments to a patient's DNA. They can also prescribe appropriate medications and dosage for a patient based on genetic sequence information. This new field is called pharmacogenetics (also pharmacogenomics), and pharmacists are helping to lead the way. In some places, it's already possible for patients to walk into a community pharmacy and ask for a pharmacogenetic test. Or people can order these tests online. At the new Preventive Genomics Clinic at Brigham and Women's Hospital in Boston, which opened in August 2019, patients can see geneticists and genetic counselors and request from a selection of genetic tests. At this concierge clinic, patients pay out of pocket and can even choose a genomic test that looks at more than three thousand genes and can cost nearly $3,000 for a full interpretation.

As researchers learn more about diseases, and as doctors factor in individual genomic information, precision medicine will offer more individualized therapies for each disease in each person.

This genetic revolution has enormous implications for health and survival. For thousands of years, modifications to the human genome occurred only through evolution. But new methods of gene transfer and gene editing have the potential to alter or replace natural selection. Societies will need to develop policies, procedures, and regulations so that genomic medicine has the greatest benefit to individuals and communities. The promise of curing previously untreatable diseases must be balanced with the dangers of unregulated uses of human genetic modification. Imagine what could happen if governments used genomic medicine to serve the interests of military domination and nationalistic power.

How will society use these powerful techniques to enhance the quality of human existence and enrich lives? How will we make sure that people have equal access to genomic medicine and that no populations are left behind? To answer these questions, we will need a community of scientific and humanitarian experts to guide the future of genetics in society.

GLOSSARY

allele: a variant or alternative sequence of a gene, which usually arises by mutation

amino acid: a building block for a protein

autosomal: located on an autosome

autosome: any chromosome that is not a sex chromosome

base pair: a set of two nucleotides that form the links between the sugar-phosphate backbones of DNA and RNA. In DNA the pairs are adenine (A) and thymine (T), and guanine (G) and cytosine (C).

carrier: a person who possesses a disease-causing allele from one parent and a normal allele from the other parent. Carriers are usually unaffected by the disease.

chromosome: a threadlike structure of DNA and proteins found in the nucleus of most living cells

codon: a sequence of three nucleotides that together form a unit of genetic code in a DNA or RNA molecule

crossing over: the exchange of genes between chromosomes that results in a mixture of parental characteristics in offspring

de novo mutation: a genetic alteration that is present in a gamete of one of the parents but not present in either parent. It can also arise as an embryo begins to develop.

deoxyribonucleic acid (DNA): a self-replicating material present in nearly all living organisms that carries heritable genetic information

diploid: containing two complete sets of chromosomes, one from each parent

DNA polymerase: a type of enzyme that helps form new copies of DNA, in the form of nucleic acid molecules during DNA replication

DNA sequencing: determining the order of nucleotides in a piece of DNA

dominant: expressed when only one copy of the allele is present

enzyme: a protein that triggers a chemical reaction in a living organism

eugenics: the discredited idea of improving the human population by controlled breeding or by selecting desired heritable traits

eukaryote cell: any cell or organism that possesses a clearly defined nucleus

exome: the part of the genome consisting of exons

exon: a part of DNA that contains instructions for making protein

gamete: a sex cell, such as an egg and sperm

gene: a basic physical and functional unit of heredity made of DNA

gene editing: the manipulation of the genetic material of a living organism by deleting, replacing, or inserting a DNA sequence

gene therapy: a therapy that either replaces a gene mutation with a corrected copy of the gene or upregulates a second gene to increase protein function

genetic disorder: a disease or condition caused by a mutation in a gene that prevents it from functioning normally

genetic linkage: the tendency of DNA sequences that are close together on a chromosome to be inherited together during the meiosis phase of sexual reproduction

genetics: the study of single genes and their role in the way traits or conditions are passed from one generation to the next

genome: an organism's complete set of DNA

genomics: a field of study within genetics concerned with the structure, function, evolution, and mapping of entire genomes

genotype: an organism's complete set of genes, or a set of alleles that determines the expression of a particular trait

germline: the gamete-producing cells in a sexually reproducing organism

germline editing: gene editing of the germline (sex) cells, which could cause DNA changes to be passed to offspring and alter the gene pool

granuloma: a mass of immune cells that forms at a site of inflammation or infection

haploid: having a single set of unpaired chromosomes

intron: a part of DNA that does not contain instructions for making proteins

karyotype: the number and visual appearance of the chromosomes in the cell nuclei of an organism or species as seen under a microscope

matrilineal: based on kinship with one's mother or female ancestors

meiosis: when a single cell divides twice to produce four haploid cells, each containing half the original amount of genetic information

messenger RNA (mRNA): ribonucleic acid (RNA) transcribed from the DNA of a gene in the cell nucleus, which provides the template for building proteins

mitochondria: complex organelles of cells that convert energy from food into a form that the cell can use. They have their own genetic material, separate from the DNA in the nucleus, and can make copies of themselves.

mitosis: a type of cell division that results in two daughter cells each having the same number and kind of chromosomes as the parent nucleus, typical of ordinary tissue growth

mutation: a DNA variation that occurs in less than 1 percent of the population

next-generation sequencing (NGS): non-Sanger-based method used to determine a portion of the nucleotide sequence of an individual's genome. It is also called massively parallel sequencing.

nucleotide: an organic molecule that is the building block of DNA and RNA

nucleus: an organelle in most eukaryote cells that contains DNA

pathogenic: capable of causing disease

patrilineal: based on the relationship to one's father or male ancestors

pharmacogenomics: the study of how genes affect an individual's response to medications

phenotype: the set of observable characteristics of an individual resulting from the interaction of its genotype with the environment; often refers to the clinical features of a disease

polymorphism: a DNA variation that exists in more than 1 percent of the population

protein: a string of amino acids linked by peptide bonds

recessive: expressed when two copies of the allele are present

Sanger sequencing: a low-throughput method used to determine a portion of the nucleotide sequence of an individual's genome

single nucleotide polymorphisms (SNPs): a variation in a nucleotide sequence that occurs in more than 1 percent of the population. Some forms of SNPs are associated with increased risk of disease.

trait: a specific characteristic of an organism

upregulate: to increase the expression of a gene

whole exome sequencing: a method to determine the DNA sequence variations in exons of genes

whole genome sequencing: a method to determine the DNA sequence variations of all regions of DNA, including both the exons and introns

SOURCE NOTES

5   Roy, interview with the authors, August 2, 2018.

5   Roy.

9   Gina Kolata, "Medical Detectives Find Their New Disease," *New York Times*, February 2, 2011.

9   NIH Undiagnosed Diseases Program, May 24, 2017, https://www.genome.gov/27544402/the-undiagnosed-diseases-program/.

12   William Gahl, interview with the authors, April 28, 2017.

13   National Institutes of Health, US National Library of Medicine, Genetics Home Reference, accessed December 10, 2019, https://ghr.nlm.nih.gov/primer/testing/genetictesting/.

13–14 Roy, interview.

14   Sydney, interview with the authors, November 6, 2018.

16   Roy, interview.

16   NIH's National Institute of Allergy and Infectious Diseases, accessed April 11, 2019, https://www.niaid.nih.gov/diseases-conditions/ctla4-deficiency/.

17   Roy, email correspondence with the authors, August 26, 2019.

24   Gian A. Nogler, "The Lesser-Known Mendel: His Experiments on *Hieracium*," *Genetics* 172, no. 1 (January 1, 2006): 1–6, http://www.genetics.org/content/172/1/1/.

26   William Bateson and Beatrice Durham Bateson, *William Bateson, F.R.S. Naturalist: His Essays and Addresses, Together with a Short Account of His Life* (London: Cambridge University Press, 1928), 458.

26–27 Bateson and Bateson.

31   Sigourney Weaver, narrator, PBS, April 23, 2003, https://www.pbs.org/wgbh/nova/transcripts/3009_photo51.html.

33   Anne Sayre, *Rosalind Franklin and DNA* (New York: W. W. Norton, 2000), 126.

35   James D. Watson, *The Double Helix: A Personal Account of the Discovery of the Structure of DNA* (New York: W. W. Norton, 1980), 98.

35   Watson, 99.

36   Watson, 115.

37   Francis Crick, "Francis Crick Dies at 88," ABC, July 30, 2004, http://www.abc.net.au/pm/content/2004/s1165891.htm.

37   "The Nobel Prize in Physiology or Medicine 1962," Nobel Prize, Nobel Media AB 2019, December 23, 2019, https://www.nobelprize.org/prizes/medicine/1962/summary/.

38   Celeste, email correspondence with the authors, October 29, 2018.

45   American College of Medical Genetics, "Newborn Screening: Toward a Uniform Screening Panel and System—Executive Summary," *Pediatrics* 117, no. 5, pt. 2 (May 2006): S296–307.

47   Kevin Alexander, email correspondence with the authors, October 29, 2018.

48   Alexander, email correspondence with the authors, January 18, 2019.

48   Alexander, email, October 29, 2018.

48   Renee, email correspondence with the authors, October 20, 2018.

49   Allen, email correspondence with the authors, October 20, 2018.

51   National Human Genome Research Institute, accessed December 18, 2015, https://www.genome.gov/10001177/dna-sequencing-fact-sheet/.

53   YourGenome.Org, accessed February 5, 2016, https://www.yourgenome .org/facts/timeline-history-of-genomics/.

58–59 National Human Genome Research Institute, October 21, 2015, https:// www.genome.gov/10000715/.

59   Charles Moore, "25th Anniversary of Cystic Fibrosis Gene Discovery Breakthrough Commemorated," Cystic Fibrosis News Today, September 18, 2014, https://cysticfibrosisnewstoday.com/2014/09/18/25th -anniversary-cystic-fibrosis-gene-discovery-breakthrough -commemorated/.

62   Ann Jurecic, "Life Writing in the Genomic Age," *Lancet*, February 27, 2014, https://www.thelancet.com/journals/lancet/article/PIIS0140 -6736(14)60394-9/fulltext.

65   Louise, interview with the authors, October 15, 2018.

65   Louise, interview with the authors, September 8, 2019.

65   Louise, interview with the authors, September 7, 2019.

73   Eric Dishman, NIH All of Us Research Program, September 25, 2018, https://allofus.nih.gov/news-events-and-media/announcements/nih -funded-genome-centers-accelerate-precision-medicine-discoveries/.

73   Stephanie Devaney, quoted on Richard Harris, "How Should Scientists' Access to Health Databanks Be Managed?," NPR, *Morning Edition*, September 6, 2019.

75   Michael, interview with the authors, September 8, 2019.

75   Louise, interview with the authors, September 8, 2019.

78   Paul Steven Miller and Rebecca Leah Levine, "Avoiding Genetic Genocide: Understanding Good Intentions and Eugenics in the Complex Dialogue between the Medical and Disability Communities," *Genetics in Medicine* 15, no. 2 (February 2013): 95–102, https://www.ncbi.nlm.nih.gov/pmc /articles/PMC3566260/.

79   National Geographic Genographic Project, December 22, 2019, https:// genographic.nationalgeographic.com/about/.

80   National Geographic Genographic Project, accessed January 17, 2020, https://genographic.nationalgeographic.com/.

80   Ann Turner, "The Meaning of Your Mutations," special report on coding region mutations, private correspondence on April 7, 2008.

81   FamilyTreeDNA Forum, July 22, 2008, https://forums.familytreedna.com /forum/general-interest/dna-and-genealogy-for-beginners/5057-mtdna -mrca/.

84   Phil Rogers, Lisa Capitanini, and Courtney Copenhagen, "Home DNA Kits: What Do They Tell You?," NBC 5 Chicago, April 30, 2018, https:// www.nbcchicago.com/investigations/home-dna-kits-481292431.html.

86   Stephany Leigh Tandy-Connor et al, "False-Positive Results Released by Direct-to-Consumer Genetic Tests Highlight the Importance of Clinical Confirmation Testing for Appropriate Patient Care," *Genetics in Medicine* 20 (2018): 1515–1521, https://www.nature.com/articles/gim201838/.

86–87   Arthur Caplan, quoted in Justin Petrone, "Controversial Ancestry Ad Reignites Discussion about Minorities and Consumer Genomics," Genomeweb.com, May 2, 2019, https://www.genomeweb.com/applied -markets/controversial-ancestry-ad-reignites-discussion-about-minorities -and-consumer/.

87   Steve Almasy and Andrea Diaz, "Ancestry.com Apologizes for Ad Criticized for Romanticizing Slavery," CNN, April 19, 2019, https://www .cnn.com/2019/04/18/us/ancestry-ad-slavery-blacklash/index.html.

87   Brian Resnick, "Genetics Has Learned a Ton—Mostly about White People. That's a Problem," Vox, October 27, 2018, https://www.vox.com/science -and-health/2018/10/22/17983568/dna-tests-precision-medicine-genetics -gwas-diversity-all-of-us/.

87   Jason White, quoted in Steve Temko, "Makers of At-Home DNA Test Kits Seek to Help Customers Cope with Surprising, Life-Changing Results," ABC, January 30, 2019, https://abcnews.go.com/living/story/makers -home-dna-test-kits-seek-customers-cope-60709941/.

88   Eli Baden-Lasar, in Pia Peterson, "He Found Out He Had 32 Siblings. For the *Times Magazine*, He Took Their Pictures," *New York Times*, June 29, 2019.

90   Ann Wojcicki, "Consumers Don't Need Experts to Interpret 23andMe Genetic Risk Reports," Stat, April 9, 2018, https://www.statnews.com /2018/04/09/consumers-23andme-genetic-risk-reports/.

90   Nancy Wurtzel, quoted in Elizabeth Richards, "Can Genetic Counselors Keep Up with 23andMe?," *Atlantic*, May 22, 2018, https://www .theatlantic.com/health/archive/2018/05/can-genetic-counselors -keep-up-with-23andme/560837/.

91   Megan Molteni, "The Future of Crime-Fighting Is Family Tree Forensics," *Wired*, December 26, 2018, https://www.wired.com/story/the-future-of -crime-fighting-is-family-tree-forensics/.

92 Jon Schuppe, "Police Were Cracking Cold Cases with a DNA Website. Then the Fine Print Changed," NBC News, October 23, 2019, https://www.nbcnews.com/news/us-news/police-were-cracking-cold-cases-dna-website-then-fine-print-n1070901/.

92 Jocelyn Kaiser, "A Judge Said Police Can Search the DNA of 1 Million Americans without Their Consent. What's Next?," *Science*, November 7, 2019, https://www.sciencemag.org/news/2019/11/judge-said-police-can-search-dna-millions-americans-without-their-consent-what-s-next/.

93 Matthew Shaer, "The False Promise of DNA Testing," *Atlantic*, June 2016, https://www.theatlantic.com/magazine/archive/2016/06/a-reasonable-doubt/480747/.

94 23andMe, email to Lily, December 6, 2013.

95 Genos, accessed January 17, 2020, https://genos.co/sequencing.html.

97 National Human Genome Research Institute, accessed October 4, 2017, https://www.genome.gov/27528684/1000-genomes-project/.

99 Stephany Leigh Tandy-Connor, quoted in "Home Genetic Tests Should Be Interpreted by Experts," Springer Nature, March 22, 2018, https://www.springer.com/gp/about-springer/media/research-news/all-english-research-news/home-genetic-tests-should-be-interpreted-by-experts/15532734/.

100 Katherine, interview with the author, February 26, 2019.

105 Amander Clark, quoted in Rachel Lehmann-Haupt, "Get Ready for Same-Sex Reproduction," Neo.Life, February 28, 2018, https://medium.com/neodotlife/same-sex-reproduction-artificial-gametes-2739206aa4c0/.

106 Jennelle Stephenson, interviewed on CBS, *60 Minutes*, March 10, 2019, https://www.cbsnews.com/news/more-on-the-trial-aiming-to-cure-sickle-cell-60-minutes/.

107 National Heart, Lung, and Blood Institute, NIH, press release, March 12, 2019, https://www.nhlbi.nih.gov/news/2019/sickle-cell-patients-recovery-after-gene-therapy-heightens-hopes-cure/.

109 Jennelle Stephenson, quoted in Hal Boedeker, "Kissimmee Woman, Rid of Sickle Cell Anemia, Feels '100 Times Better,'" *Orlando Sentinel*, March 20, 2019.

110 Francis Collins, interviewed on CBS, *60 Minutes*, March 10, 2019, https://www.cbsnews.com/news/could-gene-therapy-cure-sickle-cell-anemia-60-minutes/.

112 Jennifer Doudna, "How CRISPR Lets Us Edit Our DNA," YouTube video, 15:53, posted by TED, November 12, 2015, https://www.youtube.com/watch?v=TdBAHexVYzc/.

113 Rob Stein, "Scientists Create New, More Powerful Technique To Edit Genes," *All Things Considered*, October 21, 2019, https://www.npr.org/sections/health-shots/2019/10/21/771266879/scientists-create-new-more-powerful-technique-to-edit-genes/.

113   Stein.

114   He Jiankui, "About Lulu and Nana: Twin Girls Born Healthy after Gene Surgery as Single-Cell Embryos," YouTube video, 4:43, posted by the He Lab, November 25, 2018, https://www.youtube.com/watch?v=th0vnOmFltc/.

115   Alcino J. Silva, quoted in "Chinese Gene-Editing Scientist He Jiankui May Have Made the Twins Smarter, Scientists Say," ABC News, February 24, 2019, https://www.abc.net.au/news/2019-02-25/gene-editing-scientist -may-have-made-the-twins-smarter/10845220/.

115   He Jiankui, quoted in Pam Belluck, "Chinese Scientist Who Says He Edited Babies' Genes Defends His Work," *New York Times*, November 28, 2018, https://www.nytimes.com/2018/11/28/world/asia/gene-editing -babies-he-jiankui.html.

115   Jennifer Phillips, quoted in Katarina Zimmer, "CRISPR Scientists Slam Methods Used on Gene Edited Babies," *Scientist*, December 4, 2018, https://www.the-scientist.com/news-opinion/crispr-scientists-slam -methods-used-on-gene-edited-babies--65167/.

116   Eric Lander et al, "Adopt a Moratorium on Heritable Genome Editing," *Nature*, March 13, 2019, https://www.nature .com/articles/d41586-019-00726-5/.

116   Francis Collins, quoted in Belluck, "Chinese Scientist."

116   Hannah Osborne, "China Confirms Three Gene Edited Babies Were Born through He Jiankui's Experiments," *Newsweek*, January 2, 2020, https:// www.newsweek.com/china-third-gene-edited-baby-1480020/.

116   Francis S. Collins, "NIH Director on Human Gene Editing: 'We Must Never Allow Our Technology to Eclipse our Humanity,'" *Discover*, December 29, 2019, https://www.discovermagazine.com/health/nih-director-on-human -gene-editing-we-must-never-allow-our-technology-to/.

118–119   Dan Ming, "Female Runners with High Testosterone Must Take Hormone Suppressants to Compete, Sports Court Rules," Vice News, May 1, 2019, https://www.vice.com/en_us/article/wjvda4/female-runners-with-high -testosterone-must-take-hormone-blockers-to-compete-sports-court -rules/.

119   Caster Semenya, quoted in Rick Maese, "Court Rules Olympic Runner Caster Semenya Must Use Hormone-Suppressing Drugs to Compete," *Washington Post*, May 1, 2019, https://www.boston.com/sports/olympics /2019/05/01/caster-semenya-court-ruling-testosterone/.

119   Joshua D. Safer, quoted in Denise Grady, "Anatomy Does Not Determine Gender, Experts Say," *New York Times*, October 22, 2018.

120   Victor Mather and Jeré Longman, "Ruling Leaves Caster Semenya with Few Good Options," *New York Times*, July 31, 2019, https://www.nytimes .com/2019/07/31/sports/caster-semenya.html.

121   Wendy, interview with the authors, September 7, 2016.

122   Peter Tyson, "The Hippocratic Oath Today," *NOVA*, March 27, 2001, https://www.pbs.org/wgbh/nova/article/hippocratic-oath-today/.

SELECTED BIBLIOGRAPHY

Almasy, Steve, and Andrea Diaz. "Ancestry.com Apologizes for Ad Criticized for Romanticizing Slavery." CNN, April 19, 2019. https://www.cnn.com/2019/04/18/us/ancestry-ad-slavery-blacklash/index.html.

American College of Medical Genetics. "Newborn Screening: Toward a Uniform Screening Panel and System—Executive Summary." *Pediatrics* 117, no. 5, pt. 2 (May 2006): S296–307. Abstract available online at http://www.ncbi.nlm.nih.gov/pubmed/16735256/.

Barrett, Rebecca. Radio interview with James Watson and Francis Crick on *PM*, ABC, July 30, 2004. http://www.abc.net.au/pm/content/2004/s1165891.htm.

Bateson, William, and Beatrice Durham Bateson. *William Bateson, F.R.S. Naturalist: His Essays and Addresses, Together with a Short Account of His Life.* London: Cambridge University Press, 1928.

Belluck, Pam. "Chinese Scientist Who Says He Edited Babies' Genes Defends His Work." *New York Times*, November 28, 2018.

Boedeker, Hal. "Kissimmee Woman, Rid of Sickle Cell Anemia, Feels '100 Times Better.'" *Orlando Sentinel*, March 20, 2019.

"Chinese Gene-Editing Scientist He Jiankui May Have Made the Twins Smarter, Scientists Say." ABC News, February 24, 2019. https://www.abc.net.au/news/2019-02-25/gene-editing-scientist-may-have-made-the-twins-smarter/10845220/.

Collins, Francis. Interviewed on CBS, *60 Minutes*, March 10, 2019. https://www.cbsnews.com/news/more-on-the-trial-aiming-to-cure-sickle-cell-60-minutes/.

de Souza, Sandro J. Quoted in "What Is Known about the Function of Introns, the Nonencoding Sequences in Genes?" *Scientific American*, October 21, 1999. https://www.scientificamerican.com/article/what-is-known-about-the-f/.

di Resta, Chiara, Silvia Galbiati, Paola Carrera, and Maurizio Ferrari. "Next-Generation Sequencing Approach for the Diagnosis of Human Diseases: Open Challenges and New Opportunities." *Journal of the International Federation of Clinical Chemistry and Laboratory Medicine* 29, no. 1 (April 2018): 4–14.

Doudna, Jennifer. "How CRISPR Lets Us Edit Our DNA." YouTube video, 15:53. Posted by TED, November 12, 2015. https://www.youtube.com/watch?v=TdBAHexVYzc/.

FamilyTreeDNA Forum, July 22, 2008. https://forums.familytreedna.com/forum/general-interest/dna-and-genealogy-for-beginners/5057-mtdna-mrca/.

Galton, Francis. *Hereditary Genius*. London: Macmillan, 1892.

Grady, Denise. "Anatomy Does Not Determine Gender, Experts Say." *New York Times*, October 22, 2018.

Green, Erika L., Katie Benner, and Robert Pear. "'Transgender' Could Be Defined Out of Existence under Trump Administration." *New York Times*, October 21, 2018.

Harris, Richard. "How Should Scientists' Access to Health Databanks Be Managed?" NPR, *Morning Edition*, September 6, 2019. https://www.npr.org /sections/health-shots/2019/09/06/755402750/how-should-scientists-access -to-health-databanks-be-managed/.

He, Jiankui. "About Lulu and Nana: Twin Girls Born Healthy after Gene Surgery as Single-Cell Embryos." YouTube video, 4:43. Posted by the He Lab, November 25, 2018. https://www.youtube.com/watch?v=th0vnOmFltc/.

Kolata, Gina. "Medical Detectives Find Their New Disease." *New York Times*, February 2, 2011.

Lander, Eric, Françoise Baylis, Feng Zhang, Emmanuelle Charpentier, Paul Berg, Catherine Bourgain, Barbel Friedrich et al. "Adopt a Moratorium on Heritable Genome Editing." *Nature*, March 13, 2019. https://www.nature.com/articles /d41586-019-00726-5/.

Lehmann-Haupt, Rachel. "Get Ready for Same-Sex Reproduction." Neo.Life, February 28, 2018. https://medium.com/neodotlife/same-sex-reproduction -artificial-gametes-2739206aa4c0/.

Maese, Rick. "Court Rules Olympic Runner Caster Semenya Must Use Hormone-Suppressing Drugs to Compete." *Washington Post*, May 1, 2019.

Miller, Paul Steven, and Rebecca Leah Levine. "Avoiding Genetic Genocide: Understanding Good Intentions and Eugenics in the Complex Dialogue between the Medical and Disability Communities." *Genetics in Medicine* 15, no. 2 (February 2013): 95–102.

Ming, Dan. "Female Runners with High Testosterone Must Take Hormone Suppressants to Compete, Sports Court Rules." Vice News, May 1, 2019. https:// www.vice.com/en_us/article/wjvda4/female-runners-with-high-testosterone -must-take-hormone-blockers-to-compete-sports-court-rules/.

Molteni. Megan. "The Future of Crime-Fighting Is Family Tree Forensics." *Wired*, December 26, 2018. https://www.wired.com/story/the-future-of-crime-fighting-is -family-tree-forensics/.

Moore, Charles. "25th Anniversary of Cystic Fibrosis Gene Discovery Breakthrough Commemorated." Cystic Fibrosis News Today, September 18, 2014. https://cysticfibrosisnewstoday.com/2014/09/18/25th-anniversary-cystic-fibrosis-gene-discovery-breakthrough-commemorated/.

National Heart, Lung, and Blood Institute. NIH, press release, March 12, 2019. https://www.nhlbi.nih.gov/news/2019/sickle-cell-patients-recovery-after-gene-therapy-heightens-hopes-cure/.

Nogler, Gian A. "The Lesser-Known Mendel: His Experiments on *Hieracium*." *Genetics* 172, no. 1 (January 1, 2006): 1–6. http://www.genetics.org/content/172/1/1/.

Peterson, Pia. "He Found Out He Had 32 Siblings. For the *Times Magazine*, He Took Their Pictures." *New York Times*, June 29, 2019.

Petrone, Justin. "Controversial Ancestry Ad Reignites Discussion about Minorities and Consumer Genomics." Genomeweb.com, May 2, 2019. https://www.genomeweb.com/applied-markets/controversial-ancestry-ad-reignites-discussion-about-minorities-and-consumer/.

Resnick, Brian. "Genetics Has Learned a Ton—Mostly about White People. That's a Problem." Vox, October 27, 2018. https://www.vox.com/science-and-health/2018/10/22/17983568/dna-tests-precision-medicine-genetics-gwas-diversity-all-of-us/.

Richards, Elizabeth. "Can Genetic Counselors Keep Up with 23andMe?" *Atlantic*, May 22, 2018. https://www.theatlantic.com/health/archive/2018/05/can-genetic-counselors-keep-up-with-23andme/560837/.

Rogers, Phil, Lisa Capitanini, and Courtney Copenhagen. "Home DNA Kits: What Do They Tell You?" NBC 5 Chicago, April 30, 2018. https://www.nbcchicago.com/investigations/home-dna-kits-481292431.html.

Sayre, Anne. *Rosalind Franklin and DNA*. New York: W. W. Norton, 2000.

Shaer, Matthew. "The False Promise of DNA Testing." *Atlantic*, June 2016. https://www.theatlantic.com/magazine/archive/2016/06/a-reasonable-doubt/480747/.

Stephenson, Jennelle. Interviewed on CBS, *60 Minutes*, March 10, 2019. https://www.cbsnews.com/news/more-on-the-trial-aiming-to-cure-sickle-cell-60-minutes/.

Tandy-Connor, Stephany Leigh, Jenna Guiltinan, Kate Krempely, Holly LaDuca, Patrick Reineke, Stephanie Gutierrez, Phillip Gray, and Brigette Tippin Davis. "False-Positive Results Released by Direct-to-Consumer Genetic Tests Highlight the Importance of Clinical Confirmation Testing for Appropriate Patient Care." *Genetics in Medicine* 20 (2018): 1515–1521. https://www.nature.com/articles/gim201838.

Temko, Steve. "Makers of At-Home DNA Test Kits Seek to Help Customers Cope with Surprising, Life-Changing Results." ABC, January 30, 2019. https://abcnews .go.com/living/story/makers-home-dna-test-kits-seek-customers-cope-60709941/.

Turner, Ann. "The Meaning of Your Mutations." Special report on coding region mutations, private correspondence, April 7, 2008.

Watson, James D. *The Double Helix: A Personal Account of the Discovery of the Structure of DNA*. New York: Scribner, 1998.

Wojcicki, Ann. "Consumers Don't Need Experts to Interpret 23andMe Genetic Risk Reports." Stat, April 9, 2018. https://www.statnews.com/2018/04/09 /consumers-23andme-genetic-risk-reports/.

Yeager, Ashley. "Lack of Diversity in Genetic Datasets Is Risky for Treating Disease." *Scientist*, March 21, 2019. https://www.the-scientist.com/news-opinion /lack-of-diversity-in-genetic-datasets-is-risky-for-treating-disease-65631/.

Zimmer, Katarina. "CRISPR Scientists Slam Methods Used on Gene Edited Babies." *Scientist,* December 4, 2018. https://www.the-scientist.com/news -opinion/crispr-scientists-slam-methods-used-on-gene-edited-babies--65167/.

FURTHER INFORMATION

Books

Ballen, Karen Gunnison. *Decoding Our DNA: Craig Venter vs the Human Genome Project*. Minneapolis: Twenty-First Century Books, 2013.

Doudna, Jennifer A., and Samuel H. Sternberg. *A Crack in Creation: Gene Editing and the Unthinkable Power to Control Evolution*. Reprint, Boston: Mariner Books, 2018.

Judson, Horace Freeland. *The Eighth Day of Creation: Makers of the Revolution in Biology*. New York: Simon & Schuster, 1979.

Maddox, Brenda. *Rosalind Franklin: The Dark Lady of DNA*. New York: HarperCollins, 2002.

McKissick, Katie. *What's in Your Genes?* Avon, MA: Adams Media, 2014.

Metzl, Jamie. *Hacking Darwin: Genetic Engineering and the Future of Humanity*. Naperville, IL: Sourcebooks, 2019.

Mukherjee, Siddhartha. *The Gene: An Intimate History*. New York: Scribner, 2016.

Olby, Robert. *The Path to the Double Helix: The Discovery of DNA*. Reprint ed. New York: Dover, 2012.

Rosenberg, Leon E., and Diane Drobnis Rosenberg. *Human Genes and Genomes: Science, Health, Society*. London; Waltham, MA: Elsevier Academic Press, 2012.

Tagliaferro, Linda. *Genetic Engineering: Modern Progress or Future Peril*. Minneapolis: Twenty-First Century Books, 2010.

Films

Cracking Your Genetic Code. Produced by NOVA. Boston: WGBH and PBS, 2012.

DNA: Secret of Photo 51. Produced by NOVA. Boston: WGBH and PBS, 2007.

The Gene Doctors. Produced by Rob Wittlesey, Sean B. Carroll, and Cara Feinberg. Directed by Rob Wittlesey. Chevy Chase, MD: Tangled Bank Studios, 2017.

Websites

All of Us Research Program
> https://www.joinallofus.org/en
> The program is a historic effort to gather data from one million or more
> people living in the United States to accelerate research and improve health.

Bioethics Research Library: Genetics and Ethics
> https://bioethics.georgetown.edu/explore-bioethics/genetics-and-ethics/
> View links to resources on ethics and human genetics.

Cambrooke Therapeutics
> https://www.cambrooke.com/
> Read about nutrition therapy and products for people with serious unmet
> medical nutrition needs. Find flavorful, easy options that can help people
> sustain unique diets and maintain nutritional needs.

Cook for Love: Low Protein Recipes
> https://cookforlove.org/
> Cook for Love is a culinary project of National PKU News, a nonprofit
> organization dedicated to providing support, resources, and education to
> individuals, families, and clinicians managing phenylketonuria (PKU).

The Council for Responsible Genetics
> http://www.councilforresponsiblegenetics.org
> Read about the social, ethical, and environmental implications of genetic
> technologies.

The Embryo Project Encyclopedia
> https://embryo.asu.edu/home
> The Embryo Project is a collection of researchers who study the historical
> and social contexts of developmental and reproductive biology. The
> researchers work to communicate with inclusive audiences about
> reproductive medicine, developmental biology, and embryology.

ENCODE Project
> https://www.encodeproject.org/
> Researchers embarked on the ENCODE Project to figure out the purpose
> of the remaining 98 to 99 percent of the genome, outside of the area that
> carries genes.

Ethical, Legal, and Social Implications Research Program at NIH (ELSI)
> https://www.genome.gov/10001618/the-elsi-research-program/
> The National Human Genome Research Institute's Ethical, Legal, and Social
> Implications Research Program was established in 1990 as part of the
> Human Genome Project to foster basic and applied research on the ethical,
> legal, and social implications of genetic and genomic research for individuals
> and communities.

Genetic Timeline—National Human Genome Research Institute
https://www.genome.gov/pages/education/genetictimeline.pdf
Learn about the major steps in human genome research, beginning with
Charles Darwin in 1859 through the successes at the Human Genome
Project in 2003 to the present.

Genome: Unlocking Life's Code
https://unlockinglifescode.org/timeline
This is an online collaboration between the National Human Genome
Research Institute and the Smithsonian's National Museum of Natural
History. Explore a genomic timeline, learning tools, History Channel videos,
news article, information on genomic careers, and more. Celebrate National
DNA Day on April 25 each year.

Museum of disABILITY History
http://museumofdisability.org/exhibits/past/birth-of-newborn-screening
/the-guthrie-test/
The Museum of disABILITY History is dedicated to advancing the
understanding, acceptance, and independence of people with disabilities.
The museum's exhibits, collections, archives, and educational programs
create awareness and a platform for dialogue and discovery.

The National Human Genome Research Institute
https://www.genome.gov/
Established in 1989, the National Human Genome Research Institute began
as the National Center for Human Genome Research to carry out the role of
the NIH in the International Human Genome Project. In 1990 the HGP began
mapping the human genome and completed its work in 2003.

The National Institutes of Health
https://www.nih.gov/
The NIH, the medical research agency of twenty-seven institutes, is funded
by the US Congress and pursues health-related research and provides
training at its institute's campus in Bethesda, Maryland.

Newborn Screening Tests by State
https://www.babysfirsttest.org/newborn-screening/screening-101
Learn about newborn screening, a public health service that reaches almost
four million babies born in the United States each year.

PBS *NOVA*: Secret of Photo 51
https://www.pbs.org/wgbh/nova/photo51/
View articles, interviews, slideshows, and resources on Rosalind Franklin
and her Photo 51. Follow an animated journey into the tiny world of DNA.

PKU Podcast with Kevin Alexander
    https://pkulifepodcast.podbean.com/
    PKU Life Podcast features interviews with people who have PKU from across
    the world.

Recommended Uniform Screening Panel (RUSP)
    https://www.hrsa.gov/advisory-committees/heritable-disorders/rusp/index
    .html
    The RUSP is a list of disorders that are recommended by the secretary of the
    Department of Health and Human Services for states to screen as part of
    their state universal newborn screening programs.

SNPedia
    https://www.snpedia.com/index.php/SNPedia
    SNPedia is a wiki investigating human genetics. It shares information about
    the effects of variations in DNA, citing peer-reviewed scientific publications.
    It is used by Promethease to create a personal report linking your DNA
    variations to the information published about them.

Undiagnosed Diseases Network
    https://undiagnosed.hms.harvard.edu/
    The Undiagnosed Diseases Network is a research study backed by the NIH
    Common Fund that seeks to provide answers for patients and families
    affected by mysterious conditions.

INDEX

ABOUT THE AUTHORS

Whitney Stewart graduated from Brown University. She is an award-winning children's books author and a mindfulness instructor. As an adult, she was diagnosed with an inherited immune deficiency, and this deepened her interest in medical genetics and inspired her advocacy for patients with complicated disorders. Her most recent publication is *Mindfulness and Meditation: Handling Life with a Calm and Focused Mind*. To learn more about her work or contact her, go to www.whitneystewart.com.

Hans C. Andersson, MD, is the Karen Gore Chair of Human Genetics and director of the Hayward Genetics Center at the Tulane University Medical School, where he directs the Biochemical Genetics Lab. Following fellowship training in clinical genetics and cell biology at the National Institutes of Health and University of Gottingen, Germany, Andersson achieved American Board of Medical Genetics certification in clinical genetics and clinical biochemical/molecular genetics and American Board of Pediatrics certification in pediatrics. His research has elucidated clinical features and pathophysiology of inherited metabolic genetic disorders, especially in lysosomal storage disorders. He leads the major regional referral center for such diseases in the Gulf South and is a member of the board for the International Collaborative Gaucher Group and a member of numerous national societies including the Society of Pediatric Research and the Society of Inherited Metabolic Diseases.

PHOTO ACKNOWLEDGMENTS

Image credits: backgrounds: Olena Yepifanova/iStock/Getty Images; sefa ozel/iStock/Getty Images; anusorn nakdee/iStock/Getty Images; pialhovik/iStock/Getty Images; Lonely__/iStock/Getty Images; anusorn nakdee/iStock/Getty Images; Nobi_Prizue/iStock/Getty Images; Pallava Bagla/Corbis/Getty Images, p. 7; Science Photo Library/Getty Images, p. 10; bakdc/Shutterstock.com, p. 15; Aldona Griskeviciene/Shutterstock.com, p. 23; The Natural History Museum/Alamy Stock Photo, p. 26; A. Barrington Brown//Science Source, p. 33; Science Source, p. 34; Universal History Archive/Universal Images Group/Getty Images, p. 35; Thierry BORREDON/Gamma-Rapho/Getty Images, p. 36; Arno Burgi/picture alliance/Getty Images, p. 43; Kevin Alexander, Adult living with PKU, p. 47; Laura Westlund/Independent Picture Service, pp. 52, 54, 66, 89, 98, 111; Martin Shields/Science Source, p. 57; National Institutes of Health/Department of Health and Human Services, p. 62; Science History Images/Alamy Stock Photo, p. 68; Suzanne Kreiter/The Boston Globe/Getty Images, p. 77; Paul HANNY/Gamma-Rapho/Getty Images, p. 82; Linda Davidson/The Washington Post/Getty Images, p. 83; Science History Images/Alamy Stock Photo, p. 89; Justin Sullivan/Getty Images, p. 93; Science Picture Co/Collection Mix: Subjects/Getty Images, p. 106; Gregor Fischer/picture alliance/Getty Images, p. 117; Mark Kolbe/Getty Images, p. 118; Micheline Pelletier/Sygma/Getty Images, p. 124.

Cover: Lonely__/iStock/Getty Images; anusorn nakdee/iStock/Getty Images.